INTRODUCING ICT

Support Material

Support material for this book is available at *www.gillexplore.ie*

Support material for this book consists of solutions to assignments (available to teachers only) and data for the assignments on spreadsheets and databases.

INTRODUCING ICT

Basic to Intermediate

Teresa Walsh

Gill Education
Hume Avenue
Park West
Dublin 12
www.gilleducation.ie

Gill Education is an imprint of M.H. Gill & Co.

Design by DesignLab, Dublin
Print origination in Ireland by O'K Graphic Design, Dublin

The paper used in this book is made from the wood pulp of managed forests. For every tree felled, at least one tree is planted, thereby renewing natural resources.

Photo Credits

For permission to reproduce photographs and other material, the author and publisher gratefully acknowledge the following:
1, 4, 6, 8, 9, 27 courtesy of Hewlett Packard; 5T courtesy of Microsoft; 5B, 14 © Imagefile Ireland; 5C © Science Photo Library/Phillip Hayson; 12T © Alamy Images; 13 © Freecom.com.

The author and publisher have made every effort to trace all copyright holders, but if any has been inadvertently overlooked we would be pleased to make the necessary arrangements at the first opportunity.

For Rebecca, Simon and Sarah

CONTENTS

Acknowledgments

I would like to thank Hubert Mahony and everyone at Gill & Macmillan for their help and advice in preparing the text. Special thanks go to my former colleagues in the IT Department at St Conleth's Vocational School for their many helpful comments and suggestions. Thanks to my family and friends for their support and encouragement.

Unit 1 – Know Your Computer

In this Unit you will find information on •Computer Systems, •The Parts of a Computer, •Input Devices, •Output Devices, •Storing Data, •Computer Networks as well as Questions on the topics.

1. Computer Systems

A computer is a machine that processes data to produce information.
Everything that a computer does depends on it being told exactly what to do and how to do it. The instructions that computers use are called **programs** or **software**. There are different types of software available, known as **application software**, depending on what you want the computer to do. Word processors, spreadsheets, databases and programs to design web pages, calculate company payroll and plan driving routes are all examples of application software.

Figure 1.1: A personal computer

Input, Processing and Output

Whenever you use a computer it must work its way through three basic stages before any task can be completed. These stages are

input, **processing** and **output**. The computer uses a program to work through these stages. A program is a set of instructions, which tells the computer exactly what to do with input in order to get the required output.

Input

The input stage of computing involves getting the data needed by the program into the computer. **Input devices** are used to do this. The most common input devices are the keyboard and the mouse.

Processing

The program holds instructions about what to do with the input. During the processing stage the computer follows these instructions using the data which has been input.

Output

This stage is concerned with producing processed data as information in a form that is useful to the user. **Output devices** are used to do this. The most common output devices are the screen and the printer.

Data

Data is a collection of numbers, characters or other symbols that has been coded into a format that can be input to a computer and processed. The main **types** of data that can be input into a computer and processed are **numeric**, **text**, **dates**, **graphics** and **sound**. All data ends up being stored by the computer as a series of numbers.

Operating Systems

An **operating system** is a set of programs that controls how the hardware of a computer works. The operating system works as a means of communication between the user and the computer. It deals with the loading and running of application software and manages the transfer of data and files to and from additional devices. Some of the most common operating systems are the various versions of Windows, Mac OS (for Apple Mac computers), Novell Netware, UNIX and Linux.

2. The Parts of a Computer

Hardware is the name that is given to any part of the computer that you can touch. An individual piece of hardware, e.g. the keyboard, is called a **device**. The basic hardware of all computers has the following four parts:

- Central Processing Unit (CPU).
- Input Devices.
- Output Devices.
- Backing Store Devices.

Figure 1.2: The parts of a computer

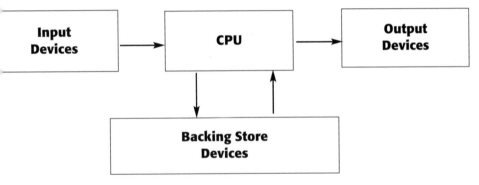

Central Processing Unit (CPU)

The **CPU** is the part of the computer where data is manipulated e.g. calculations are made and searches and sorting are done. The CPU contains the **Main Memory**, the **Control Unit** and the **Arithmetic and Logic Unit (ALU)**.

Main Memory

The main memory holds the program instructions and data. It contains two types of memory chips called **ROM** and **RAM**.

Control Unit

The control unit takes instructions from the main memory, interprets them and sends them to the ALU to be implemented.

↓

Arithmetic and Logical Unit (ALU)

The ALU performs calculations and makes decisions using these instructions.

3. Input Devices

Input devices are used to get the data needed by the program into the computer. Different devices are used depending on the kind of data to be entered.

Keyboard

The **keyboard** is the most common way of manually inputting text and numbers into a computer. Ordinary computer keyboards have their keys arranged in a similar way to those on a typewriter. This method of arranging the keys is called **QWERTY** because of the order in which the keys appear on the first row of letters (see Figure 1.3). Computer keyboards also have extra keys that can do different tasks depending upon the software that is being used.

Figure 1.3: Layout of keys on standard QWERTY keyboard

Some computer keyboards have a very different layout and set of keys because of the special tasks for which they have been designed. The keys on the keyboard of a supermarket till are a good example of this; take a close look at them the next time you go shopping!

Mouse

After the keyboard, the **mouse** is the next most common method of manually inputting data. The user moves a mouse around on a flat surface next to the computer. When a mouse is moved around, a small ball underneath it turns and sends information to the computer. **Mouse driver** software uses this information to move a small arrow around the screen. All mice have at least two buttons; the left button is usually used to make selections.

Trackball

Figure 1.5: A trackball attached to a keyboard

A **trackball** is usually attached to the keyboard and has buttons beside it, which do the same as the buttons on a mouse. The user turns the trackball with a finger to move the cursor around the screen. The trackball saves the space normally taken up by the mouse and the mouse mat.

Touch Pads

Figure 1.6: A touch pad on a laptop computer

These are **touch sensitive devices** usually an inch or two square that replace the mouse. When the user touches the surface the result is similar to using a mouse or trackball.

They are often used instead of a mouse on laptop computers.

Scanner

A **scanner** can be used to input text, pictures, graphics or images into a computer. Scanners work by passing a beam of very bright light over an image. There are different types of scanners, the most common are found in shops and supermarkets and are used to read the bar codes on products, which then show the details on the cash register.

Another type of scanner is the **flatbed scanner** (see figure 1.7). Once an image has been scanned on this type of scanner it can be edited and saved using special software.

Figure 1.7: A flatbed scanner

Digital Camera

Like all cameras a **digital camera** takes still photographs, but rather than store them on film they are stored electronically as an image file. The main advantage of this is that an image file can be read by a computer straight away – bypassing the need for developing and scanning. A digital camera stores images in computer memory which can be erased and reused. Most models have removable memory cards.

Figure 1.8: A digital camera and memory cards

Disk Drives

Data can also be input from floppy disks, CD and DVD disks, as well as from a number of removable drives that can be connected to the computer.

Other manual input devices include; **joysticks** for computer games, **touch screens** e.g. tills in fast-food outlets, **microphones** to input sound into a computer and **light pens** for graphic applications.

Table 1.1: Summary of input devices

Summary of Input Devices

Device	Speed	Advantages	Disadvantages	Where Used
Keyboard	Slow	• Most users are familiar with it	• Slow • Error prone	• Text/data entry
Mouse	Fast	• Easy to use	• Limited pointing device	• GUI-based software
Trackball	Fast	• Easy to use • Less space needed	• Limited pointing device	• GUI-based software
Touchpad	Fast	• Easy to use • Less space needed	• Limited pointing device	• GUI-based software
Scanner (Flatbed)	Fast	• Easy to use • Fast (no keying)	• Uses a lot of memory	• DTP • Word Processing
Digital Camera	Fast	• Easy to use • No developing • PC not required • Easy manipulation of pictures • Erase bad pictures	• Expensive ongoing costs • Poor picture quality on some models • Time consuming	• Home • School • Work

4. Output Devices

Before a computer can produce any output it must have an **output device** connected to it. The main output devices that are used to get output from a computer are:

Monitor

The **monitor** or **visual display unit** (VDU) is an output device that accepts a video signal direct from the computer. The size of a monitor is measured in inches diagonally across the screen; 15-, 17-, 19- and 21-inch monitors are the most common sizes.

The picture on a monitor is made up of thousands of tiny dots called pixels going across and down the screen. The quality and detail of the picture depends on the resolution the monitor is capable of displaying.

Figure 1.9: A monitor

The quality of the image on a monitor is also affected by its **refresh rate**. This is measured in **hertz** (Hz) and indicates how many times per second the image on the screen is updated. To have flicker-free images, thus avoiding headaches and eyestrain, the refresh rate of a monitor should be at least 75 Hz.

Printers

A **printer** is a device that produces a printout or **hard copy** of information from a computer. There are many different types of printers to choose from. Which one you pick will depend on:

- How much you want to pay.

- The cost of the ink that it uses.

- The quality of the print you want.

The most common types of printer are **inkjet** and **laser**.

Inkjet Printers

An **inkjet printer** forms characters and graphics on a page by producing patterns of tiny dots from very small openings in the print head. The cost of ink cartridges for some low-priced inkjets can make the less expensive model more expensive to operate in the long run. However, inkjet printers are the ideal printer for the home where printing volume is usually small.

Figure 1.10: An inkjet printer

Large-format inkjet printers are used to produce the final output for commercial posters and **Computer Aided Design (CAD)** output.

Laser Printers

Laser printers give very high-quality printed output of both text and graphics very quickly and very quietly. The laser printer not only produces hard copy faster than any other type of printer, but the laser printed pages are more sharply detailed. They are generally more expensive to buy than inkjet printers and the toner cartridges are more expensive, but they are ideal where the print volume is high.

Figure 1.11: A laser printer

Thermal Printers

There are two types of thermal printers: **direct thermal** and **thermal wax transfer**. The direct thermal printer prints the image by burning dots onto coated paper as it passes over the heated printhead. Direct thermal printers are increasingly replacing the dot matrix printer because of their higher print speed and substantially quieter operation. Thermal wax transfer printers use a thermal transfer ribbon that melts a coloured wax onto paper creating almost photo-realistic images.

Speakers and Headphones

Figure 1.12: Headphones

Computers can output music, voices and other sounds using **speakers** or **headphones**. To be able to output sound in the first place a computer needs to have a special circuit board called a **sound card** inside it. The quality and volume of the sound produced by a computer can be improved by connecting **external speakers** into a port on your computer. Headphones can also be attached to a port so that only the person using the computer can hear the sound.

Table 1.2: Summary of output devices

Summary of Output Devices

Device	Speed	Advantages	Disadvantages	Where Used
Monitor	Fast	• Immediate results	• Temporary display • Radiation emisssions	• Temporary output
Inkjet Printer	Slow	• Good quality • Cheap to buy • Quiet	• Expensive to run • Slow	• Low-volume high-quality output
Laser Printer	Fast	• Excellent quality • Fast • Quiet	• Expensive to run	• Large volume • Excellent quality output
Speakers		• Produce sound	• Noisy in classroom setting	• When sound is required
Headphones		• Noise control	• Damage to hearing	• For individual sound needs

5. Storing Data

The programs and data needed by a computer are stored using data storage devices. Data storage devices can be divided into two main categories: main memory and backing storage.

Main Memory

Computers store and process data using **binary numbers**. Binary numbers are used by computers because it is very simple to make electronic circuits for them. This is because a binary number is represented by a pattern of **0's** and **1's** – 1 means 'on' and 0 means 'off'. From this simplest of all numeric systems, your computer can construct:

■ Representations of millions of numbers.

■ Any word in any language.

■ Hundreds of thousands of colours and shapes.

A single unit in binary is called a **bit** – this stands for **b**inary dig**it**.
    Computer memory is measured in **bytes**, with **eight bits** making up one byte. One byte can store one character e.g. 'A'. In

Table 1.3 one complete byte is shown. This byte contains the binary code that is used to represent the capital letter A.

Table 1.3: Binary code for capital 'A'

1	0	0	0	0	0	1	0

The size of a computer's memory is usually measured in kilobytes (**KB**), megabytes (**MB**) or gigabytes (**GB**). Table 1.4 shows how computer memory is measured.

Table 1.4: Measuring computer memory

1,024	Bytes in a Kilobyte
1,048,576	Kilobytes (1024 × 1024) in a Megabyte
1,073,741,824	Megabytes (1024 × 1024 × 1024) in a Gigabyte

ROM

ROM stands for **Read Only Memory**. The programs and information stored in ROM are permanent and cannot be changed. This kind of memory is used to store the instructions which the computer needs to start up. When the computer is switched off the information is not lost, it is available for the next time the computer is switched on.

RAM

RAM stands for **Random Access Memory**. RAM is the computer's work area, where it keeps the programs and data that you are working on. The information stored in RAM is not permanent and the contents of RAM are lost when a computer is switched off. That is why you should always save your work before you shut down.

Backing Storage

Backing storage is used to store programs and data when they are not being used or when the computer is switched off. Examples of backing storage devices are discussed on the following pages.

Hard Disks

Hard disks are normally found in the hard disk drive inside the computer. However, some hard disk drives are not permanently fixed inside the computer and are removable. Hard disks can store very large quantities of information and the data can be accessed very quickly. A typical hard disk can hold several gigabytes of data.

Figure 1.13: Hard disk

Floppy Disks

A **floppy disk** is a small disk made of flexible plastic that is coated with a magnetic material and protected with a hard plastic cover. The standard 3.5-inch disk can store up to 1.44 MB of data. Floppy disks are cheap and are a convenient way to get data from one PC to another.

Figure 1.14: Floppy disk

Zip Disks

Zip disks look similar to floppy disks but can store more information. A zip disk can hold up to 250 MB of data, which is approximately 170 times more than a floppy disk. They are ideal for storing large files such as graphics, video clips and audio files. They can be written to and changed.

Figure 1.15: Zip disk

USB Flash Drives

Figure 1.16: USB card

USB flash is one of the smallest and most convenient storage devices available. They are really simple things consisting of just a small memory chip that can be wrapped in a case not much bigger than packet of chewing gum. They are robust and reliable and an ideal way of backing up important files or transferring files between computers. Some flash drives include security password protection and encryption preventing others from accessing your data. They are available with many different storage capacities ranging from 32 MB up to 1 GB.

CD-ROM

CD-ROM or **Compact Disk Read-Only Memory** looks just like a music CD. Like a music CD, computer CD-ROMs store vast amounts of information. A standard CD-ROM can store approximately 650 MB of data, which is four hundred times more than a floppy disk. CD-ROM disks come with information already on them and are **read-only**. This means your computer can retrieve only the information that was on the CD when you got it, your computer can't write your own data or files to these disks.

CD-R

CD-Rs are **recordable** CDs. They are blank when you buy them and are ideal for storing music, images, data and backup files. CD-R can be recorded onto once, giving you a permanent method of storage that can't be wiped by accident. A standard CD-R can store up to 700 MB of data.

CD-RW

CD-RWs are recordable and **re-recordable** CDs. In other words you can write data to them any number of times you like. They are ideal for storing large amounts of music, images and files. A standard CD-RW can store up to 700 MB of data.

DVD-ROM

DVD-ROM stands for **Digital Versatile Disk Read-Only Memory**. DVDs look like CDs but have an enormous advantage in terms of capacity over CDs. DVDs are double-sided, compared to CDs which are single-sided. Because of their storage capacities they can hold interactive material, audio and video as well as data. DVD drives can read most CD media as well. DVD-ROM disks come with information already on them and are **read-only**. This means your computer can retrieve only the information that was on the DVD when you got it, your computer can't write your own data or files to these disks.

DVD-R

DVD-Rs are **recordable** DVDs. They are blank when you buy them and are ideal for storing movies, music and backup files. DVD-R can be recorded onto **once**, giving you a permanent method of storage that can't be wiped by accident. A standard single-sided DVD-R can store up to 4.7 GB of data.

DVD-RW

DVD-RWs are recordable and **re-recordable** DVDs. This means you can record over and over again to the same DVD. They are ideal for storing movies, music, images and files. A standard single-sided DVD-RW can store up to 4.7 GB of data.

Figure 1.17: An assortment of CDs and DVDs

Magnetic Tape

Magnetic tape can store large amounts of data and is cheap and although it is a dying technology it is still used by a lot of organisations for these reasons.

Direct and Serial Access

Hard disks, floppy disks, zip disks, CD and DVD-ROM all allow **direct access** to data. This means that the required data can be found straight away without having to read through all the data on the disk. Magnetic tape allows only **serial access** to data. This means that to locate data it has to wind through the tape from the beginning until the requested files are found. This makes it slow to find and transfer data to and from magnetic tape.

File Compression

File Compression is used so that files can be made smaller the result being that more data can be stored in the same amount of space. It is also possible to send large files via the Internet faster because a compressed file is much smaller than an original file.

    File compression software is needed to compress a file and before you can use a compressed file it has to be **decompressed**. This can be done using **decompression software** or by setting files up to be **self-extracting** which means they can automatically decompress themselves. The most common compressed files are those with extensions such as '**.zip**', '**.sit**' and '**.tar**'. An example of software that can be used to compress and decompress files is **WinZip**.

Table 1.5: Summary of storage devices

Summary of Storage Devices

Device	Access Speed	Approx. Capacity	Where Used
Hard Disc	Fast	• Varies	• All computers
Floppy Disk	Very Slow	• 1.44 MB	• Any computer with a floppy disk drive
Zip Disk	Slow	• Up to 250 MB	• Any computer with an internal or external Zip drive
Flash Drives	Fast	• Up to 1 GB	• Any computer with a USB port
CD-ROM	Fast	• Up to 700 MB	• Any computer with an internal or external CD drive
DVD-ROM	Fast	• Up to 4.7 GB on a single-sided DVD	• Any computer with an internal or external DVD drive
Magnetic Tape	Varies	• Up to 40 GB	• Any computer with an internal or external tape streamer

6. Computer Networks

A computer network is two or more computers that are linked together so that they can share hardware, software and data. A central computer called a **file server** is used to store application software and the users' files which can be accessed from any workstation on the network. Users can also share additional devices such as printers and scanners. There are two different sorts of computer networks. Local Area Network (**LAN**) – including Wireless LANs (**WLAN**) – and Wide Area Network (**WAN**).

LAN

In a **Local Area Network** (LAN) the computers are all on the same site. The computers in a LAN are all connected to each other with special cables. Most school networks are LANs.

WLAN

Wireless networking is a technology that enables two or more computers to communicate using standard network protocols, but without network cabling. WLANs are growing in popularity with businesses as it allows workers to access the LAN from remote locations and are useful in places where network wiring is impossible.

WAN

In a **Wide Area Network** (WAN) the computers are spread over a big geographical area e.g. in a town, county or across different continents. Computers in a WAN are connected using telecommunication lines and satellite links. When a computer uses an ordinary telephone line to connect to another computer a modem is needed at each end of the link.

Modem

A **modem** – or **mo**dulator **dem**odulator – is the piece of equipment required to allow two computers to communicate with each other over ordinary telephone lines. Computers generate **digital signals** that are made up from binary patterns of 0's and 1's. These signals can't be transmitted along ordinary telephone lines. A modem is used to convert the digital signal to an equivalent **analogue signal** so that it can be sent down a telephone line. At the other end, another modem is needed to convert the analogue signal back to a digital signal so that the receiving computer can interpret the signal (figure 1.18).

The speed of a modem is measured in **bits per second** (bps), which is a measure of how fast it can transfer data. Modern modems have speeds of 56,000 bps but that's only for downloading and only on a perfect phone line. Modems are needed less and less these days because modern telephone lines such as ISDN and Broadband can carry digital signals directly.

Figure 1.18: Exchanging data between computers using a telephone line and modem

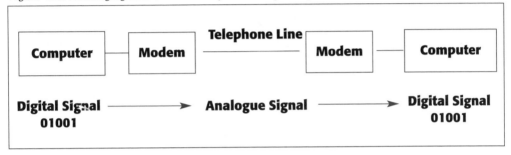

ISDN

An **Integrated Services Digital Network** (ISDN) transmits voice and data at the same time in digital format. ISDN allows data to be transferred faster than via a normal telephone line (e.g. speeds up to 128,000 bps can be achieved). ISDN allows multiple devices such as fax, telephone and computer to share the same line.

ADSL

An **Asymmetric Digital Subscriber Line** (ADSL) also transmits data in digital format but is much faster than ISDN, with speeds starting at around 512,000 bps. ADSL works by splitting your existing telephone line in two, one for voice and the other for data. The word 'asymmetric' means that the information flowing into a computer (or download) is much faster than the information flowing out of it (or upload). With ADSL you are permanently connected to the Internet but because ADSL works over normal lines you can use your telephone at the same time for analogue calls.

7. Questions

1. Name three different types of application software.
2. List the three basic stages that any computer must work through before any task can be completed.
3. Explain what is meant by the term 'data'.
4. Give examples of two different types of data.
5. Explain what is meant by the term 'operating system'.
6. Name three different operating systems.
7. Explain what is meant by the term 'hardware'.
8. Describe briefly the role of the 'central processing unit' (CPU).
9. Give three examples of input devices.
10. Mrs Carolan is going to buy a new computer and has asked for your advice about the input devices that she will need.
    (a) Name two input devices that Mrs Carolan should expect to receive as part of any standard computer package. Explain briefly why each of these devices will be needed.
    (b) Name two other input devices, which it might also be useful for Mrs Carolan to consider buying. In each case explain carefully why Mrs Carolan should consider the extra expense of having these input devices.
11. Give three examples of output devices.
12. Name two types of printer.
13. Give two advantages of laser printers.
14. What is the name given to the circuit board that produces sound in your computer?
15. How many bits are there in one byte?
16. How many bytes would be needed to store one character of text data?
17. A computer system has two types of memory, RAM and ROM.
    (a) What does RAM stand for?
    (b) What does ROM stand for?
    (c) Give two differences between RAM and ROM.
    (d) Give one use of RAM.
    (e) Give one use of ROM.
18. Put the computer memory sizes listed below into increasing order of size with the smallest first and biggest last:
    20 MB   100 KB   6 GB   60 MB   600 KB
19. What do the letters CD-ROM stand for?
20. Explain the term 'read-only'.
21. What do the letters 'DVD-ROM' stand for?

22. Explain the terms 'recordable' and 're-recordable'.
23. Give two advantages of DVD-RWs.
24. Give two advantages of 'flash drives'.
25. Explain the difference between 'direct access' and 'serial access'.
26. Explain the term 'file compression'.
27. What do the terms 'LAN' and 'WAN' stand for?
28. What is the difference between 'LAN' and 'WLAN'?
29. Explain the function of a file server.
30. Explain the term 'ISDN'.
31. Explain the term 'ADSL'.

On-line Tasks

1. Visit **www.makeitsecure.ie**
   (a) Read the article 'Useful tips to stay secure online'.
   (b) Read the article 'What is a virus?'.
   (c) Prepare a summary of both articles.
2. Visit the Free On-Line Directory of Computing (FOLDOC) at:
   http://wombat.doc.ic.ac.uk/foldoc/
   (a) Look up definitions of the keywords that are highlighted in this Unit.
   (b) Prepare a summary list of keywords and definitions for revision.
3. Visit the computer history museum at
   www.computerhistory.org
   (a) Research the history of computers.
   (b) Construct a time line to summarise your findings.

Unit 2 – Word Processing

1. Introduction to Word Processing

Word processing is a really useful program that allows you to type words, sentences and paragraphs onto a page. Then you can format the text in many different ways in order to make it look more attractive. You can add tables, charts, pictures and graphs to a document and also print addresses on envelopes and labels.

The best thing about word processing is that if you make a mistake you can easily correct it and better still the program can even correct your spelling and grammar for you if you so wish.

All word processing packages have many special features in common, which can be used to improve both the appearance and quality of printed text.

Word Processing Features

Font Size

This function allows the size of any part of the text to be changed by changing its **point size**. The larger the point size, the bigger the text will be.

This text is point **size 12**

This text is point **size 16**

Font Style

This option allows the style of any part of the text to be changed. The font styles that are available will depend on the word processor that you are using. Each different font style has its own special name.

This font is called Arial.

This font is called Broadway.

𝕿𝖍𝖎𝖘 𝖋𝖔𝖓𝖙 𝖎𝖘 𝖈𝖆𝖑𝖑𝖊𝖉 𝕺𝖑𝖉 𝕰𝖓𝖌𝖑𝖎𝖘𝖍 𝕿𝖊𝖝𝖙.

Bold, Italic and Underline

Other effects that can be used to change the appearance of text are options to make it **bold**, *italic* or <u>underlined</u> (or any combination of these).

Justification

This feature adds extra spaces to a block of text to line it up in a particular way. Text can be:

Left justified - this means that each line of text is lined up on the left-hand side only.

This text is **left** justified.

Right justified - this means that each line of text can be lined up on the right-hand side only.

This text is **right justified**.

Centred - this means that each line of text is lined up in the centre of the page and is often used for headings and titles.

This text is **centred**.

Fully justified - this means that each line of text is lined up on both the left- and right-hand sides of the page, like some books. This paragraph is fully justified.

Word processing packages often show similar functions like these together on a toolbar to make them easier to use. Figure 2.1 shows the **formatting toolbar** of Microsoft Word which is a popular word processing package.

Figure 2.1: Formatting toolbar of a popular WP package

Word-wrap

This means that when you are entering text you do not have to press the **Enter** key at the end of a line; the word processor will begin a new line whenever one is needed. The Enter key is only pressed to start a new paragraph or to leave a deliberate gap of one or more lines between blocks of text.

Cut, Copy and Paste

The cut facility of a word processor allows you to choose a part of your text and 'cut it out'. 'Cut' text can either be thrown away or **pasted** back onto the page in a different place. The **copy** facility allows you to select part of your text and then paste a copy of it elsewhere in your document. The cut, copy and paste facilities of a word processor can be used with graphics in a similar way to text.

Find and Replace

Find and replace allows you to tell the word processor to look for one word and replace it with another. This can be done **selectively** for just part of a document or **globally**. Selective find and replace will check each time it finds the search word whether or not you want it replacing. Global find and replace just finds every occurrence of the search word and replaces it without asking first.

Figure 2.2: Using Find and Replace

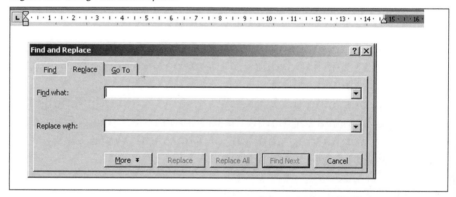

Line Spacing

Line spacing is used to change the amount of space between lines of text. Normal text is single-spaced.

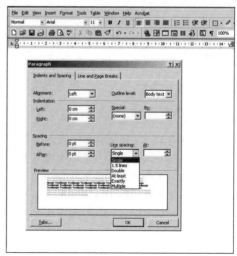

Figure 2.3: Changing line spacing

Spell Checkers

A spell checker uses a built-in dictionary to check the spellings in your text. When a spell checker finds words that are unknown, it will offer possible alternatives from its dictionary and ask if you want to choose a replacement, delete the unknown word completely, keep the word as it is, or enter your own alternative word. Spell checkers are not foolproof, however, and you do need to have a reasonable knowledge of correct spellings, otherwise you might end up choosing incorrect alternative words as corrections. Figure 2.4 shows a spell check facility being used. The dialogue box shows incorrect spellings and suggests possible words to use as corrections.

Figure 2.4: Using a spell check facility

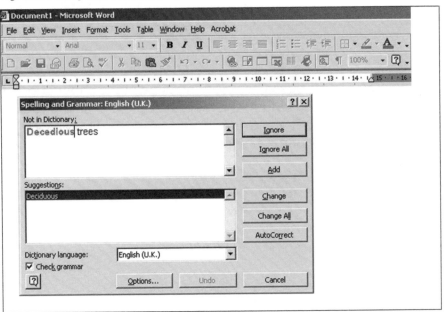

Grammar Checkers

A grammar checker uses a built-in set of rules about the grammar of the language that you are using. Grammar checkers do not check spellings; they just check that what you have written follows the rules of a language correctly.

Figure 2.5: Using a grammar check facility

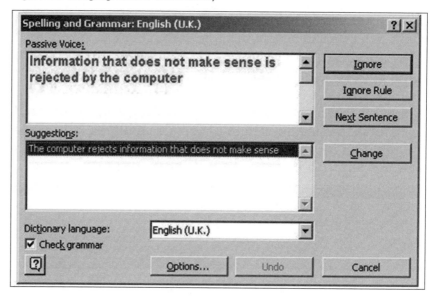

Margins

Margins refer to the space between the edge of the paper and the start of the text. The width of the margins can be changed to suit the type of document you are going to produce. There are four margins called: top, bottom, left and right.

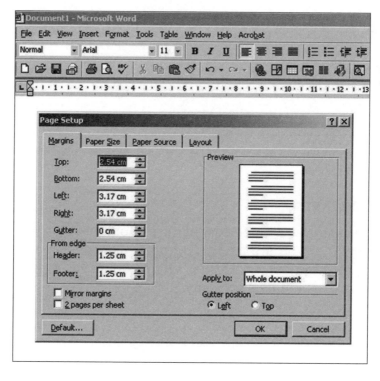

Figure 2.6:
Setting up the
margins in a
popular WP
package

Bullets and Numbering

When entering a list of items you can get the computer to automatically create a **numbered** list or a **bulleted** list. Most word processing packages have a large range of bullet and number formats to choose from.

Figure 2.7: Choosing a bullet style

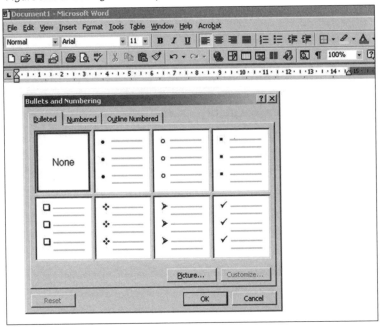

Headers and Footers

Headers and **Footers** contain text and/or graphics that appear at the top and/or bottom of every page. Headers are used a lot to show chapter numbers in books and Footers are generally used to insert page numbers.

Importing and Exporting

One of the best features of word processing is that it allows you to import graphics and combine graphics with text. What this means is that diagrams and pictures produced using other software packages can be included on the page along with your text. The **import** facility is the feature that makes this possible. The **export** facility is simply the opposite of import. Export allows you to transfer work produced using the word processor into other software packages.

Graphics

There are two basic types of graphics that you can use in word processing documents: **drawing objects** and **pictures**.

Drawing objects produce images that are made up from lines and shapes such as circles, squares and rectangles. These objects can be enhanced with colours, patterns, borders and other effects. They are referred to as **Vector Graphics** and can be stretched, scaled and resized without distortion.

Pictures and photographs downloaded from the Internet, retrieved from a CD-ROM, taken with a digital camera or a scanner, and clipart are saved in a different way from vector graphics. File formats include .bmp, .gif, .jpg and .tif (these suffixes are added to the filename automatically when the file is saved). You can insert these files into your documents and then change and enhance the pictures. These pictures are referred to as **Bitmap Graphics**.

Tabulation

This allows the **tab key** to be set to jump forward a pre-set distance across the page each time it is pressed. The user can set up the distance the tab key will jump to any value required.

Page Orientation

Page orientation refers to the way the page is facing when it is printed. Most pages are printed in a **Portrait** (vertical) direction. **Landscape** (horizontal) is useful if you want to print a lot of text on a page, e.g. a spreadsheet with a lot of columns.

Portrait

Landscape

Mail Merging

This is a special feature that is included in most word processing packages. It allows the user to create a standard letter and then merge it with data from a spreadsheet, database or other text file. This file is called the source data file. During the merging process data from fields in individual records in the source data file is inserted into spaces that have been specifically marked in the standard letter. So a personalised letter is produced for each record in the source data file.

Mail merging is a very quick method of producing letters containing virtually the same information except for the names and addresses of the people in each letter. Only one standard letter has to be written in order to produce many mail-merged copies.

Entering Text

On opening a word processing application you will be presented with a blank document. Where the cursor flashes is called the **insertion point**. This is where text will appear if you start to type.

Before you start to type, however, you need to have a look at the keyboard layout.

Your keyboard will look like this:

Figure 2.8: The keyboard

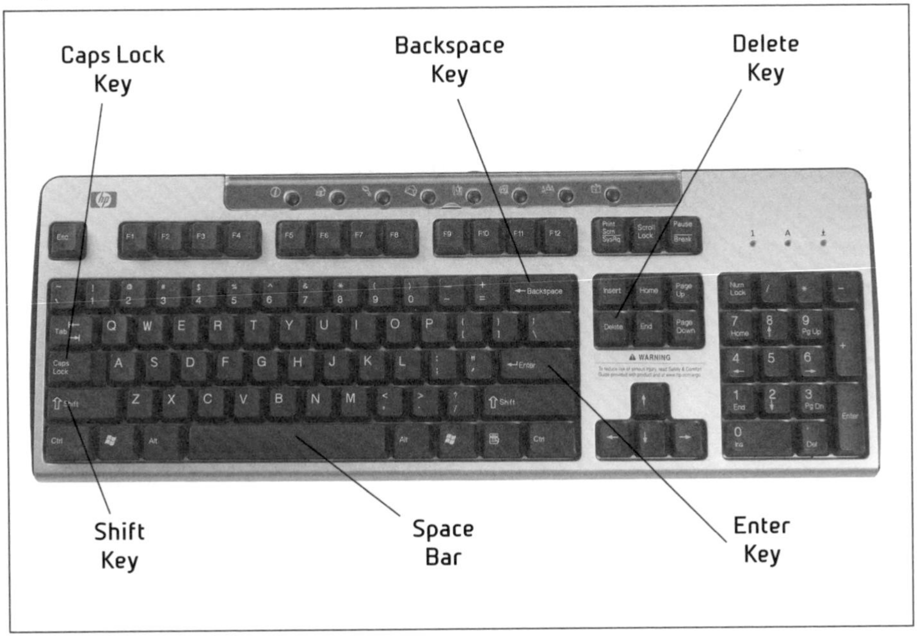

Caps Lock Key

Backspace Key

Delete Key

Shift Key

Space Bar

Enter Key

Some of the keys have been labelled on the diagram, here is some information on what they do.

The **Space Bar**. This is used to make a space between words.

The **Shift** key. As long as you hold this down all the letters you type will be in capitals. If a key has two symbols, you will type the top one.

The **Cap Locks** key. If you want a whole sentence to be in capitals, you can use the Caps Locks key. Just press it once and release it. All the letters you type after that will be capitals. Press **Cap Locks** again when you want to stop typing capitals.

The **Backspace** key. This deletes the letters to the left of where the cursor is flashing. If you are typing something and press a wrong letter, pressing **Backspace** will delete it and you can then type the right letter.

The **Delete** key. This deletes the letter to the right of where the cursor is flashing. It is not as useful as the **Backspace** key for correcting mistakes as you are going along, but you will find it comes in useful.

The **Enter** key. Use this when you want to go to a new line. There are two **Enter** keys on the keyboard, one marked with a bent arrow the other marked **Enter**. They both do exactly the same thing. People who are typing lists of numbers like to use the one near the numbers and people who are typing text like to use the one near the letters.

2. Word Processing Assignments 1–29

Assignment 1

In Assignment 1 you will: **•Enter text •Change font size •Format text (bold, italic and underline) •Justify text (centre) •Save.**

Figure 2.9

> The Ocean
>
> The Ocean is a huge area of salt water that covers most of the Earth's surface. It is split into five main parts: the Pacific, Atlantic, Indian, Southern and Arctic oceans. Some oceans have smaller parts called seas.
>
> The water in the oceans is always moving. At the surface, the wind whips the water into waves that crash onto the land. Deep down, warm and cold rivers of water called currents, flow through the oceans of the world.

 Tip

Remember to use the **Shift** key for capital letters.

 Note

In order to make changes to text you have already typed, you have to select it first – when text is selected, it shows up highlighted white on a black background.

Task 1
Open a new document and enter the text in figure 2.9 using font size 14.

Task 2
Centre the heading **The Ocean**, change it to bold format and underline it.

Task 3
Put the words **Pacific, Atlantic, Indian, Southern** and **Arctic** in italics.

Task 4
Put the word **currents** in bold.

Task 5
Save the document as **OCEANS**.

 Tip

Look at the top of your screen. Once you have saved your work you should see the name of the document there.

Assignment 2

In Assignment 2 you will: **•Enter text •Change font size •Format text (bold, italic and underline) •Justify text (centre and full) •Spell check •Save.**

Task 1
Open a new document and enter the text in figure 2.10 using font size 14.

Figure 2.10

Forests

A forest is a large area of land where lots of trees grow together. Tropical rainforests grow near the Exuator, where it is hot and wet all year round.

Confierous and deceduous forests grow in cooler places that have warm summers and cool winters. Forests are home to people and all kinds of wildelife.

Task 2

Centre the heading **Forests**, change it to bold format and underline it.

Task 3

Fully justify the rest of the text.

Task 4

Use the spell checker to check the spelling of the document and make any necessary corrections.

Task 5

Put the words **Tropical**, **Equator**, **Coniferous** and **Deciduous** in italics and bold.

Task 6

Save the document as **FOREST**.

Assignment 3

In Assignment 3 you will: •**Open existing file** •Insert new paragraph •Format text (bold and italic) •Justify text (full) •**Change font type** •Spell check •Save.

Task 1

Open the document called **FOREST**. (Assignment 2)

Task 2

Enter the text in figure 2.11 as a new paragraph.

 Tip

To get a new line press the **Enter** key.

Figure 2.11

Trees that grow in coniferous forests have waxy, green needle-like leaves that stay on the branches all year round. Conifer seeds grow in woody cones. Most of the wood that is used to build homes and make paper comes from conifers such as pine and spruce.

Task 3
Put the words **pine** and **spruce** in bold and italics and fully justify the new paragraph.

Task 4
Use the spell checker to check the spelling of the paragraph you have added and make any necessary corrections.

Task 5
Change the font of the whole document to **Arial**.

Task 6
Save as **FOREST2**.

Assignment 4

In assignment 4 you will: •Enter text •Change font size •Format text (bold, italic and underline) •Justify text (centre) •Spell check •**Cut and Paste** •Save •**Print**.

Task 1
Open a new document and enter the text in figure 2.12 using font size 12.

Tip

It's always a good idea to save your work every few minutes.

Figure 2.12

River

The end of a river is called the **mouth**. When a river flows into the ocean, the fresh river water mixes with the salt water.

The start of a river is called the **source**. As a river flows down a mountain it carves out a deep **valley** in the land.

A river is a large stream of fresh water that flows into another river, a lake, or the ocean. A river usually begins high in the mountains then flows downhill.

Task 2
Select the first paragraph and cut it out.

Task 3
Paste the first paragraph after the last paragraph.

Task 4
Select the second paragraph and cut it.

Task 5
Paste the second paragraph before the first paragraph.

Tip

Preview your page before printing to make sure that your printout will be what you expect.

Task 6
Use the spell checker to check the spelling and make any necessary corrections.

Task 7
Save as **RIVER** and print one copy.

Assignment 5

In assignment 5 you will: •Enter text •**Insert symbol (@)** •Change font size, style and **colour** •Format text (bold, italic and underline) •Justify text (centre) •**Copy and Paste** •Spell check •Save •Print.

Task 1
Open a new document and enter the text in figure 2.13 using font size 14.

Tip

Type the text first using **left-alignment** and then arrange it on the page how you want it.

Figure 2.13

Computer Solutions
Church View, Leadmore, Co. Galway
Tel 091 998789 **Fax** 091 998777
E-mail CS@leadmore.ie

SALES: PC's, Laptops – (PC's built to match your specifications and budget, plenty of special offers)

UPGRADES: RAM, graphic cards, DVD, CD re-writers, hard-drives, monitors, etc

ACCESSORIES: Floppy disks, CD-R, CD-RW, mice, keyboards, modems, scanners, printers, headphones, etc

SELECTION OF USED PC'S AND LAPTOPS ALSO AVAILABLE

A LOCAL RESPONSE TO YOUR COMPUTING NEEDS

Task 2
Change the font size of the first line to size 18 and change the colour of the font to blue.

Task 3
Copy the first line and paste it before the last line.

Task 4

Change the font type of the whole document to one of your choice.

Task 5

Use the spell checker to check the spelling and make any necessary corrections.

Task 6

Save the document as **ADVERT** and print one copy.

Assignment 6

In assignment 6 you will: •Enter text •Change font size and colour •Format text (bold and italic) •Justify text (centre) **•Change line spacing •Insert picture** •Spell check •Save •Print.

Task 1

Enter the text in figure 2.14 using font size 20 and set the line spacing to 1.5.

Figure 2.14

Cake Sale
Monday 1st December
P.E. Hall

11 a.m.

Chocolate Logs
Mini Christmas cakes
Mince Pies
Novelty Cakes

And lots, lots more!

Proceeds in aid of St. Vincent de Paul

Task 2

Change the font size of the first line to 48 and the second line to 36.

Task 3

Make the poster more attractive (but legible) by using different colour fonts throughout.

 Tip

Pale colours are hard to read on a white background.

Note

To load pictures
you may need to
have the
software CD in
the drive.

Task 4
Insert a suitable picture of your choice.
Task 5
Use the spell checker to check the spelling and make any necessary corrections.
Task 6
Save as **POSTER** and print one copy.

Assignment 7

In assignment 7 you will: •Enter text •Change font size and colour •Format text (bold and italic) •Justify text (centre) •Change line spacing •Insert picture •Spell check •Save •Print.

Task 1
Create a poster similar to the one in figure 2.14 but for a school Civies Day (no-uniform day).
Task 2
Make sure you include important information on the poster e.g. date, cost and for what cause the event is raising money.
Task 3
Make the poster attractive but legible by using different size and colour fonts.

 Note

The little squares
surrounding a
picture are called
handles – when
the squares are
visible the picture
is selected.

Task 4
Insert a suitable picture.
Task 5
Save the poster as **CIVIES** and print one copy.

Assignment 8

In assignment 8 you will: •**Set Margins** •Enter text •Change font size, type and colour •Format text (bold and italic) •Insert symbol ☎ •Justify text (centre) •Insert picture •Spell check •Save •Print.

Figure 2.15

 **THE RAILWAY HOTEL**

LEADMORE

☎ **091 999046**
****

CREAM OF VEGETABLE SOUP
OR
CAESAR SALAD WITH CAJUN CHICKEN
OR
BREADED MUSHROOMS WITH GARLIC DIP

****

ROAST STUFFED TURKEY AND HAM
WITH CRANBERRY SAUCE
OR
GRILLED 8OZ STEAK WITH PEPPER SAUCE
OR
ASIAN NOODLE & VEGETABLE
STIR FRY

All the above are served with vegetables & potato of the day

****

BAILEYS CHEESECAKE
OR
FRESH FRUIT PAVLOVA
OR
APPLE PIE WITH VANILLA ICE CREAM

****

TEA OR COFFEE

€26.00

Figure 2.15 shows a sample menu from The Railway Hotel in Leadmore.

Task 1
Enter the text in figure 2.15 using font size 12 and set all the margins at 2 cm.

Task 2
Change the heading to font size 16 and make the menu more

 Note

A margin is the white space between the edge of the page and the text – margins can be changed to give a different look to your page.

attractive by using colour and by changing the font type.

Task 3

In the desserts section delete the line 'APPLE PIE WITH VANILLA ICE CREAM' and insert a new line with 'TIRAMASU GATEAU' at the top of the desserts section.

Task 4

Insert a suitable picture at the bottom of the menu.

Task 6

Save as **MENU** and print one copy with your name on it.

Assignment 9

In assignment 9 you will: •Set Margins •Enter text •Change font size, type and colour •Format text (bold and italic) •Justify text (centre) •**Bullet points** •Change line spacing •Insert picture •Insert symbol (☎, @) •Spell check •**Find and replace** •Save •Print.

Task 1

Enter the text in figure 2.16 using font size 12, font type Arial and set all margins at 2.5 cm.

Figure 2.16

ADVENTURE DAYS AND FUN WEEKENDS

EXPERIENCE THE GREAT OUTDOORS AT LEADMORE ADVENTURE CENTRE
For Bookings Telephone 091 998365

Rock Climbing
Archery
Kayaking
Windsurfing
Hill Walking
Mountain Biking

And lots, lots more!

LEADMORE ADVENTURE CENTRE
ESKER ROAD, LEADMORE, CO. GALWAY

☎ 091 998365
E-mail: adventure@Leadmore.ie

Task 2

Change the font size of the first line to 22 and make the font colour orange.

Task 3

Change the font colour of the second line to green.

Task 4

Change the rest of the document to font size 14.

Task 5

Put a bullet point before each activity.

Task 6

Insert a suitable picture.

Task 7

Change the whole document to double line spacing

Task 8

Use the Find and Replace facility to find the word 'Leadmore' and replace it with the word 'Ballybay' throughout the document.

Task 9

Save as **BAC** and print one copy with your name on it.

 Tip

You can add bullets **before** typing a list instead of after typing.

 Note

Find and Replace allows you to tell the word processor to look for one word and replace it with another.

Assignment 10

In assignment 10 you will: •Enter text •Change font size and colour •Format text (bold and **subscript**) •Justify text (centre) •**Numbered points** •Change line spacing •**Insert footer** •Spell check •Find and replace •Save •Print.

Task 1

Enter the text in figure 2.17 using font size 12.

Figure 2.17

The Water Cycle

The Sun heats water in the oceans and on land.

The warm water turns into a gas called water vapour and mixes with the air.

High in the sky, water vapour cools and turns back into water droplets. These form clouds.

Rain falls from clouds on to the ground.

Water on land flows back to the oceans.

Task 2
Centre and underline the heading and make it size 18, colour blue.
Task 3
Change the rest of the document to font size 14.
Task 4
Make each paragraph a numbered list.
Task 5
Change the line spacing of the numbered paragraphs to 1.5.
Task 6
Insert your name as a footer.
Task 7
Use the Find and Replace facility to find the word 'water' and replace it with the word 'H2O' throughout the document except for the title.
Task 8
Change the word 'H2O' to 'H_2O' throughout the whole document.
Task 9
Save as **WATER** and print one copy.

Assignment 11

In assignment 11 you will: •Enter text •Change font size, type and colour •Format text (bold, italics and underline) •Justify text (centre) •Bullet points •Change line spacing •Insert footer •Spell check •Save.

 Tip

You can use some colour if you like!

Task 1
Enter the text in figure 2.18 using font size 14. Set the left margin at 2.5 cm and all other margins at 2 cm.

Figure 2.18

VARIOUS CATEGORIES OF WRITTEN TEXT

ARGUMENT
This is where the writer tries to convince the reader as to the truth of an idea or a point of view by trying to fault the opposing point of view.

INFORMATION
Where the writer sets out to give information on a particular subject. School and College textbooks are good examples of this type of writing.

LITERATURE
Poetry, Plays and Novels are all works of the imagination mainly read for pleasure.

NARRATION
This is simply the telling of a story whether true or fictional.

PERSUASION
Where writers try to point out the positive aspects they support or the negative ones they oppose.

Task 2
Change the font type of the whole document to Courier and the line spacing to 1.5.

Task 3
Centre, bold and underline the first line and make it size 20.

Task 4
Bold and italicise the headings and create a new paragraph for each one.

Task 5
Put a bullet point before each heading.

Task 6
Insert a footer with your name and today's date.

Task 7
Save as **ENGLISH** and print one copy.

Assignment 12

In assignment 12 you will: •Enter text •Change font size, type and colour •Format text (bold and italics) •Justify text (centre) •**Insert shape (♦)** •**Insert Borde**r •**Shade border** •Bullet and numbered points •Spell check •Save •Print.

Figure 2.19

West Coast Railways

March Madness
(Offer valid Mon–Thurs only, during the month of March)

We are offering all our customers an exciting day out in Dublin. Relax in first class while you travel into our capital city and enjoy complimentary refreshments en route.
With this offer you can choose to:

- ✦ Cruise in Dublin Bay aboard a luxury yacht and savour a complimentary lunch with wine included (subject to favourable weather conditions).
- ✦ Take an open-top tour of the city and stop off at various historic locations.
- ✦ Visit the Zoological Gardens and the Phoenix Park.
- ✦ Choose one of the following activities in the afternoon:
  - ▪ Shopping in City Centre.
  - ▪ Visit the National Gallery.
  - ▪ Visit the National Museum.

- ✦ Return home in first-class luxury and comfort.

You have a choice of weekday departure times:

Departure Times

1. 07:00, 08:00 or 09:30 from Leadmore
2. 07:30, 08:30 or 10:00 from Mill Hill
3. 08:00, 09:00 or 10:30 from Deryvale

All for only €40.00 per person (Subject to availability)
Dublin ♦ Deryvale ♦ Mill Hill ♦ Leadmore

Tip

You can change the bullet symbols if you like!

Task 1
Create the advertisement as shown in figure 2.19. Set all the margins at 2 cm.
Task 2
Put a border around the first and last lines and shade the background in a colour of your choice.
Task 3
Increase the font size of the first and last lines.
Task 4
Change the font size, font style and colour of the second line.
Task 5
Put a border around the section on departure times and insert a suitable picture below that section.
Task 6
Cut the third line 'Offer valid Mon–Thurs only, during the month of March' and paste it under the picture you inserted.
Task 7
Save the advertisement as **RAILWAY** and print one copy.

Assignment 13

In assignment 13 you will: •Enter text •Set margins •**Use preset tabs** •**Insert date** •Format text (bold) •Justify text (left and centre) •Spell check •Save •Print.

Task 1
Enter the text in figure 2.20 using font size 12. Set the left margin at 3 cm and all other margins at 2.5 cm.

Figure 2.20

Tip

Don't use the space bar at all. Use the **Tab** key to move across the page – sometimes you will have to press the **Tab** key a number of times.

---

14 Avonmore Drive
Leadmore
Co. Galway

Mr John James
Manager
One Stop Shop
Leadmore
Co. Galway

Dear Mr James

Re: Deli Assistant

I would like to apply for the above position as advertised in the Leadmore Leader yesterday and enclose my Curriculum Vitae for your attention.

I am honest, hardworking and punctual and would appreciate your consideration for this post. I look forward to hearing from you.

Yours sincerely,

Thomas Smith

Task 2
Insert a new line after the last line of Thomas Smith's address and use the word processor to automatically insert today's date.

Task 3
Key in the text 'I am available for interview at any time and' after the first sentence of the second paragraph.

Task 4
Save the document as **DELI** and print one copy.

Assignment 14

In assignment 14 you will: •Enter text •Set margins •Use preset tabs •Insert date •Format text (bold) •Justify text (left and centre) •Spell check •Save •Print.

Figure 2.21 shows an advertisement that appeared in the Southern Star newspaper.

Figure 2.21

> ### – WANTED –
>
> ### Part-time Checkout Operators
>
> Applicants must be friendly and outgoing with the ability to work on own initiative. No previous experience necessary as full training will be given.
>
> Apply in writing with Curriculum Vitae to:
>
> Samantha Jones
> Sam's Supermarket
> Main Street
> Newtown
> Co. Carlow

Task 1
With the information given in Figure 2.21 open a new document and write a letter applying for the job. Look at the letter you did in Assignment 13 and use it to help you do this one.
Task 2
Use the spell checker to check the spelling in the letter and make any necessary corrections.
Task 3
Save the document as **CHECKOUT** and print one copy.

Assignment 15

In assignment 15 you will: •**Set tabs** •Enter text •Set margins •Insert date •Format text (bold) •Justify text (left and centre) •Spell check •Save •Print.

Keane's Car Sales are placing an advertisement in their local newspaper. The following information is being sent to the newspaper.

Figure 2.22

Keane's Car Sales
Church Street
Leadmore
Co. Galway
Tel 091 999345
Fax 091 999346

Tip
Never use spaces to try and line things up in columns – always use Tabs.

Leadmore Leader
Mountain View
Leadmore
Co. Galway

Dear Sir,

Please include the following information in the advertisement as discussed yesterday.

MAKE	MODEL	TYPE	COLOUR	MILES
FORD	KA	1.3 3DR	RED	21K
FORD	FOCUS	1.4LX 4DR	SILVER	20K
OPEL	ASTRA	1.4GL 4DR	BLUE	40K
OPEL	CORSA	1.2 AUTO	GREEN	19K
FORD	MONDEO	1.8LX 5DR	BLUE	25K

Yours faithfully,

John Keane
Sales Manager

Task 1
Set tabs at 1 cm, 3 cm, 6 cm, 10 cm and 13 cm.
Task 2
Set the left margin at 2.5 cm and the right margin at 2 cm and enter the text in figure 2.22 using font size 12.
Task 3
Use the word processor to automatically insert today's date in a suitable position.

Task 4

Use the cut and paste functions to cut the last line and paste it between the information on Ford and Opel cars, so that all the information on Ford cars is together.

Task 5

Save the document as **CARS** and print one copy.

Assignment 16

In assignment 16 you will: •Set tabs •Enter text •Set margins •Change font size and colour •Format text (bold) •Justify text (centre) •**Insert header** •Insert picture •Spell check •Save •Print.

Figure 2.23 shows the team lists for the first year soccer blitz.

Task 1

Set the left and right margins at 2 cm.

Task 2

Set tabs at 1 cm, 6 cm and 11 cm.

Figure 2.23

📄 *Note*

Headers appear in the top margin of printed documents – they can be made up of text, pictures and shapes.

First Year Soccer Blitz
Monday 6th November

Team Lists

Red Team	**Blue Team**	**Green Team**
John Smith	Christy Walsh	Pat Dolan
Rory O'Connor	Laura Heneghan	James Fahy
Aisling Jones	Darren Horan	Shauna Dunne
Sam Freeman	Eoin Moran	Ian Durcan
John James	Aoife Dolan	Eva Lonergan
Danny Conway	Simon Walsh	Ronan Carolan

Purple Team	**Brown Team**	**Orange Team**
Mat Foye	Shane Wilson	Jane Forde
Kevin Neary	Tom Kenny	Noel Early
Teresa Murphy	Kate Monaghan	Lily Aitken
Dara Tougher	Justin McCarthy	Jessie Nolan
Elaine Moran	Paul Kemmy	Pat Ivers
Michael Forde	Sheila Hynes	Andy Kelly

Task 3

Enter the text in figure 2.23 using font size 14.

Task 4

Change the font size of the first line to 36, the second line to 20, the third line to 26 and put them in bold format.

Task 5

Put the team names in their own colours (e.g. Make the font colour of the Red Team red, Blue Team blue etc.).

Task 6

Insert a suitable picture at the end.

Task 7

Insert the line 'Proceeds in aid of Our Lady's Hospital for Sick Children, Crumlin' after the picture. Centre, italicise the line and make it bold.

Task 8

Insert a header with your name.

Task 9

Save as **BLITZ** and print one copy.

Assignment 17

In assignment 17 you will: •Set tabs (**leader characters and decimals**) •Enter text •Set margins •Change font size and type •Format text (bold) •Justify text (centre) •Insert header •Insert picture (**as watermark**) •Spell check •Save •Print.

Figure 2.24 shows the price list for the school shop.

Task 1

Set all the margins at 2 cm.

Task 2

Set tabs at 2 cm and 12 cm. Use leader characters and decimals for the second tab stop.

Figure 2.24

Price List

Tayto	€0.45
Nutri Grain	€0.60
Snickers	€0.65
Toffee Crisp	€0.60
Coke (Can)	€0.70
Fanta (Can)	€0.70

Onion Rings	€0.45
Skips	€0.45
Crunchie	€0.70
Animal Bar	€0.20
Twix	€0.70

Task 3

Enter the text in figure 2.24 using font size 14.

Task 4

Centre the heading 'Price List' and make it bold, change the font to size 48 and the font type to one of your choice.

Task 5

Insert a suitable picture and show it as a watermark behind the text.

Task 6

On the price section of the list change the line spacing to double, increase the font size and apply bold format.

Task 7

Insert a header with your name.

Task 8

Save as **SHOP** and print one copy.

📄 *Note*

Watermarks are text or pictures that are printed faintly behind the main body text.

Assignment 18

In assignment 18 you will: •Set margins •Enter text •**Insert table** •**Vertical alignment** •Change font size and type •Format text (bold) •Justify text (centre) •Insert header •Spell check •Save •Print.

Figure 2.25 shows the opening hours at Leadmore House and Gardens.

Tip

Tables are a handy way of arranging information in neat columns.

Figure 2.25

Opening Hours May–Sept		
Month	**Day**	**Time**
May	Sat and Sunday only	2–5 p.m.
June	Daily	2–5:30 p.m.
July and August	Daily	11:30 a.m.–5:30 p.m.
September	Sat and Sunday only	2–5 p.m.

For further information telephone 091 999765

Task 1

Set all the margins at 2.5 cm.

Task 2

Centre and make bold the first two lines and make the font size 16.

Task 3

Insert a table, enter the data using font size 12 and change the vertical alignment of the text in each cell to centre.

Task 4

Centre, italicise and make bold the last line.

Task 5

Create a header and insert the following name and address:

Leadmore House and Gardens
Esker Road
Leadmore
Co. Galway

Task 6

Centre the header; make the first line bold, font size 20 and the rest font size 16.

Task 7

Save as **HOURS** and print one copy.

Assignment 19

In assignment 19 you will: •Enter text •Insert table •Vertical alignment •Change font size, type and colour •Format text (bold and italics) •Justify text (centre) •**Merge cells** •Insert header •Spell check •Save •Print (**landscape orientation**).

Figure 2.26 shows an example of a school timetable.

 Note

Landscape orientation means the page is printed sideways. With Portrait orientation the page is printed lengthways like a page in this book.

Figure 2.26

Time	Monday	Tuesday	Wednesday	Thursday	Friday
09:00–09:40	Irish	Maths	CSPE	Religion	Business
09:40–10:20	English	English	Maths	Geography	Geography
10:20–11:00	Maths	Irish	English	English	Irish
11:00–11:10	Morning Break				
11:10–11:50	History	Business	Irish	Maths	History
11:50–12:30	Geography	Business	History	Irish	English
12:30–1:10	Business	Science	SPHE	Woodwork	Maths
1:10–2:00	Lunch Break				
2:00–2:40	Woodwork	French	Sport	Science	PE
2:40–3:20	Woodwork	French	Sport	Science	Science
3:20–4:00	Religion	PE	Sport	French	French

Task 1

Insert a table in a document and create the timetable in figure 2.26. You can enter your own timetable if you want.

Task 2

Change the vertical alignment of the text in each cell to centre.

Task 3

Centre, make bold and italicise the column headings.

Task 4

Merge the cells in the 'morning break' row and the 'lunch break' row. (Do not include the 'time' cell.)

Task 5

Make the table more attractive by changing the font size, type and colour throughout.

Task 6

Insert a header with your name and your class name.

Task 7

Save as **TIMETBL** and print one copy in a landscape orientation.

Assignment 20

In assignment 20 you will: •Enter text •**Use column layout** •Change font size •Format text (bold) •Justify text (centre) •Insert header •Spell check •Save •Print.

Students at Leadmore Community College produced the newsletter in figure 2.27.

Figure 2.27

Tip

Type the text first without columns and then change the layout to columns.

Sports News

Girls Soccer

Leadmore Girls soccer team performed very well in the annual Galway 5-a-side tournament held at Leisure Land. They were narrowly beaten 0–1 by Renmore College in a tense and exciting final. The team can be very proud of their achievement emerging so successfully from a tournament where quality play featured largely throughout the day.

Athletics

Training will take place on the track at 4:15 p.m. every Monday and Thursday. Anyone who is interested is welcome to attend. Full gear must be worn.

Basketball

Congratulations to Shauna Dunne who has been selected to play in the Irish Schools Team. We wish her and the team every success.

Task 1
Create the newsletter in figure 2.27. Change the text if you wish and report on your own school's sports news.

Task 2
Create a header and insert the title using font size 16. Centre and bold the header.

Task 3
Type the text first without columns using font size 12. When you are happy with the text, change the layout to columns.

Task 4
Save as **SPORTS** and print one copy.

Assignment 21

In assignment 21 you will: •Enter text •Use column layout •Change font size •Format text (bold) •Justify text (centre) •Insert header •Insert pictures •Spell check •Save •Print.

Figure 2.28: Please note that each of the three columns continues over the page

School Tour

On Wednesday, 22nd September fifty students and five teachers, Miss Smith, Miss Jones, Mr Connolly, Mr Broderick and Mr McHale travelled on the school tour to Barcelona.

 We were blessed with beautiful weather and on our second day there travelled to 'Port Aventura' a vast theme park. This was a day of non-stop

Monastery, which lies among the rounded crags of the Montserrat Massif. The drive up the mountain was fascinating and the views of the surrounding Catalan countryside were remarkable. While in Barcelona we also visited the local aquarium, the church of 'La Sagrada Famila' started in the 1880s by Gaudi but never completed. We also visited the Noucamp Stadium home of Barcelona FC and also

shopping district. It was a remarkable five days which afforded us an excellent opportunity to learn about a different culture by sampling their food, enjoying some local entertainment and listening to the language while also having some fun. I'm sure the memories of the tour will stay with us forever. Thanks to Mr McHale for organising a great

excitement and fun, which everyone thoroughly enjoyed. Over the next few days we visited Montserrat managed to fit in some shopping in Barcelona's very fashionable tour and to all the teachers and students who made it possible.

Students at Leadmore Community College who travelled on the school tour produced a flyer to inform students, staff and parents about the trip.

Task 1
Create the flyer in figure 2.28 and insert suitable pictures. You may change the text if you wish and report on your own school tour or another event that took place.

Task 2
Create a header and insert the title using font size 16. Centre and make bold the header.

Task 3
Type the text first without columns using font size 12. When you are happy with the text, change the layout to columns.

Task 4
Save as **TOUR** and print one copy.

Assignment 22

 Tip

There are four basic steps in setting up a mail merge:
1. Create the letter.
2. Create the list of names and addresses.
3. Insert the merge fields in the letter.
4. Merge the file containing the names and addresses with the letter.

In assignment 22 you will: •Enter text •Insert header •Change font size •Format text (bold and italics) •Justify text (centre) •**Mail merge** •Spell check •Save •Print.

The letter in figure 2.29 will be sent to the members of the Board of Management using the mail merge facility.

Figure 2.29

St John's School
Avondale
Co. Cork
Tel 083 235765
Fax 083 235766

<DATE>

<TITLE> <FIRSTNAME> <SURNAME>

```
<ADDRESS1>
<ADDRESS2>
<ADDRESS3>
<COUNTY>

Dear <TITLE> <SURNAME>

I am pleased to announce that our annual Christmas Play
aptly entitled 'Santa's Elves' will be taking place on 16th
December at 8:00 p.m. in the school Gymnasium.

Please find enclosed two tickets for this event; Light
refreshments will be served afterwards. I look forward to
seeing you there.

Yours sincerely

Mrs Joan Kenny
Principal
```

Task 1
Create the letter (without merge fields) in figure 2.29.
Task 2
Insert a header with the school details.
Task 3
Centre the header, make the first line font size 16 and bold.
Task 4
Save the letter as **PLAY**.
Task 5
Create a data file with the following names, addresses and dates.
Save it as **BOM**.

 Note

It doesn't matter
if one or more of
the address lines
are blank.

Mr Danny Roache 32 Park Road Avondale Court Avondale Co. Cork 10th December	Mrs Jena Davis 'Highlands' Crossways Avondale Co. Cork 10th December
Mr Tom Smith 56 Church View Avondale Co. Cork 10th December	Mr David O'Rourke Knockridge Avondale Co. Cork 10th December

Task 6

Insert the merge fields in the main document (figure 2.29 shows you where to put them).

Task 7

Merge the data file with the main document and print one of the letters.

Assignment 23

In assignment 23 you will: •Enter text •Insert header •Insert picture •Change font size •Format text (bold) •Justify text (centre) •Mail merge •Spell check •Save •Print.

The letter in figure 2.30 will be sent to people who are being called for interview for the part-time post of Checkout Operator at Sam's Supermarket.

Figure 2.30

Sam's Supermarket

Main Street
Newtown
Co. Carlow
Tel 809 675567/Fax 809 675568
E-mail samssuper@xyz.ie

<DATE OF LETTER>

<TITLE> <FIRSTNAME> <SURNAME>
<ADDRESS1>
<ADDRESS2>
<ADDRESS3>
<COUNTY>

Dear <TITLE> <SURNAME>

Re: Part-time Checkout Operators

With reference to the above post, please attend for interview on <date> at <time>.

Please confirm by telephone or e-mail that you will be able to attend.

Yours sincerely

Samantha Smith
Proprietor

Task 1
Create the letter (without merge fields) in figure 2.30.
Task 2
Create a header with the supermarket details and insert a suitable picture.
Task 3
Centre the header, make the first line font size 16 and bold.
Task 4
Save the letter as **MARKET**.
Task 5
Create a data file with the following information and save it as **PARTTIME**.

28th February	28th February	28th February
Mr Dara Diver	Miss Jane Forde	Miss Tina Deal
231 Rowan Park	34 Eyre Road	12 Clyde Close
Newtown	Larksmeade Est.	Ravenspark
Co. Carlow	Ellis Hill	Co. Carlow
	Co. Carlow	
6th March	6th March	6th March
12:30 p.m.	1:00 p.m.	1:30 p.m.
28th February	28th February	
Mrs Eilis Dear	Mr John Kenny	
9 Connell Road	Brackley Hill	
Old Connell	Newtown	
Newtown	Co. Carlow	
Co. Carlow		
6th March	6th March	
2:00 p.m.	2:30 p.m.	

Task 6
Insert the merge fields in the main document (figure 2.30 shows you where to put them).
Task 7
Merge the data file with the main document and print one of the letters.

Assignment 24

In assignment 24 you will: •Enter text •Insert header •Insert picture •Change font size •Format text (bold) •Justify text (centre) •Mail merge •Create mailing labels •Spell check •Save •Print.

Figure 2.31

Keane's Car Sales

**Church Street
Leadmore
Co. Galway
Tel 091 999345
Fax 091 999346**

Tip

Try using
paragraph
spacing when
you type a letter
instead of leaving
a blank line
between
paragraphs.

<DATE>

<TITLE> <FIRSTNAME> <SURNAME>
<ADDRESS1>
<ADDRESS2>
<ADDRESS3>
<COUNTY>

Dear <FIRSTNAME>

Re: Your Order

We are pleased to inform you that the <MAKE> <MODEL>, <TYPE>
in <COLOUR> that you ordered will soon be arriving in our
showroom.

It will be ready for collection on <DAY> at <TIME>. As previously
agreed the balance <PRICE> is due when you collect the car. We
look forward to seeing you then.

Yours sincerely,

John Keane
Sales Manager

The letter in figure 2.31 is being sent to some people who have
ordered cars at Keane's Car Sales.

Task 1
Create the letter (without merge fields) in figure 2.31.
Task 2
Create a header with the garage details and insert a suitable
picture.
Task 3
Centre the header, make the first line font size 20 and bold.

Task 4

Save the letter as **SALES**.

Task 5

Create a data file with the following information and save it as **ORDER**.

16th January	16th January	16th January
Mr Jimmy King	Ms Rita Jones	Mr Darren Day
The Laurels	15 King Street	'Highfields'
Dumbfield	Leadmore	Birches Lane
Leadmore	Co. Galway	Leadmore
Co. Galway		Co. Galway
Ford	Opel	Ford
Focus	Astra	Mondeo
1.4LX 4DR	1.4GL 4DR	1.8LX 5DR
Mint	Azure	Black
19th January	20th January	19th January
10:00 a.m.	10:00 a.m.	10:30 a.m.
€17,000	€19,500	€23,000

Task 6

Insert the merge fields in the main document (figure 2.31 shows you where to put them).

Task 7

Merge the data file with the main document and print one copy of each letter. Save this file as **SALELETTERS**.

Task 8

Create mailing labels for the letters and save the labels as **ORDERLABELS**.

Assignment 25

In assignment 25 you will: •**Use drawing toolbar** •**Insert text boxes** •Enter text •Format text (bold) •Justify text (centre) •**Fill colour** •Save •Print.

Tip

If the type of label you want to use is not listed in the selection box, you might be able to use one of the other listed labels – or you may be able to create your own custom labels.

Figure 2.32

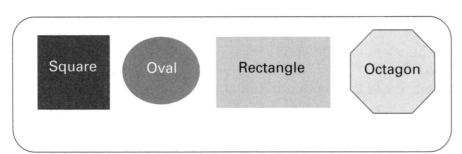

Square   Oval   Rectangle   Octagon

Task 1

Using the drawing toolbar insert the shapes in figure 2.32 on a page.

Task 2

Insert a text box in each shape and enter the name in each one.

Task 3

Fill each shape with a different colour.

Task 4

Insert a header with your name.

Task 5

Save as **SHAPES** and print one copy.

Assignment 26

In assignment 26 you will: •Use drawing toolbar (AutoShapes and WordArt) •Insert text boxes •Insert picture •Enter text •Insert bullet points •Format text (bold and italics) •Justify text (centre) •Save •Print.

Figure 2.33

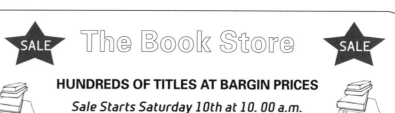

HUNDREDS OF TITLES AT BARGIN PRICES

Sale Starts Saturday 10th at 10. 00 a.m.

- Children's Books
- Gardening Books
- Computer Books

- School Books
- Travel Books
- Lots, lots more

Task 1

Using the drawing toolbar create the flyer in figure 2.33.

Task 2

Make the flyer more attractive by using colour, changing the font sizes and font types.

Task 3

Insert a header with your name.

Task 4

Save as **SALE** and print one copy.

Assignment 27

In assignment 27 you will: •Use drawing toolbar (AutoShapes and WordArt) •Insert text boxes •Insert picture •Enter text •Insert bullet points •Format text (bold and italics) •Insert table •Justify text (centre) •Insert border •Save •Print.

Figure 2.34 shows an advertising flyer that is being sent out to all homes in the Leadmore area.

Figure 2.34

Guess
where Santa is getting his bike this Christmas?
at

Casey Cycles

Main Street, Leadmore. Tel 091 999348

Caring for our customers for over 50 years

- Raleigh
- Saxon
- Trek
- Reflex

- Gary Fisher
- Dawes
- Falcon
- British Eagle

Order your bicycle before 1st December and choose from one of the following free gifts: Helmet (value €20), Speedometer, Basket, and Stopwatch.

Berg Go-Karts

Lights from €20

December Opening Hours	
Monday–Friday	9 a.m.–9 p.m.
Saturday	9 a.m.–6 p.m.
Sunday	2 p.m.–6 p.m.
Closed 25th, 26th, 27th and 31st December	

We've got the **Largest Selection**, the **Lowest Prices**, and the **Best Repair Service** around.

Battery Operated Motorcycles now in stock

Casey Cycles

Task 1

Create the flyer. You can use a different picture and use your own words and design if you wish.

Task 2

Make the flyer more attractive by using colour, changing the font sizes and font types.

Task 3

Put a Christmas themed border around the whole flyer.

Task 4

Insert a header with your name.

Task 5

Save the flyer as **CASEYXMAS** and print one copy.

Assignment 28

📄 *Note*

Vector graphics can be stretched, scaled and resized without distortion.

Figure 2.35 shows a logo that was produced for Avondale Ice Cream using Vector Graphics.

Task 1

Create the logo in figure 2.35 using vector graphics.

Figure 2.35

Task 2

Make the logo more attractive by using colour in it.

Task 3

Save the logo as **AICLOGO**.

Task 4

Print one copy of the logo.

Task 5

Create a logo using vector graphics for a music company or a computer company of your choice. You can make up the name if you wish.

Assignment 29

Figure 2.36 is an advertisement for Avondale Ice Cream that has been created using Clip Art, WordArt, text and AutoShapes.

Task 1

Create the advertisement for Avondale Ice Cream as seen in figure 2.36 and insert the company logo that you created in assignment 28.

Figure 2.36

Task 2

Make the advertisement more attractive by using colour throughout.

Task 3

Save the advertisement as **AICADD** and print one copy.

Task 4

In assignment 28 you created a logo for a company. Now create an advertisement to promote that company using a combination of Clip Art, pictures, WordArt, text and AutoShapes.

Unit 3 - Spreadsheets

1. Introduction to Spreadsheets

A spreadsheet is a really useful piece of software that is mainly used for working with numbers. Spreadsheets are used in lots of different applications that involve doing calculations or drawing charts on data such as:

- Daily or monthly average temperatures.
- Planning budgets and working with financial data.
- Marks for a class of pupils.

On opening a spreadsheet application, you will be presented with a screen that is made up of **rows** (across) and **columns** (down). Each row has its own number (1, 2, 3 ...) and each column has its own letter (A, B, C ...). The point at which rows and columns meet is called a **cell** and this will be indicated by the cell pointer. Look at figure 3.1 to see this.

Figure 3.1

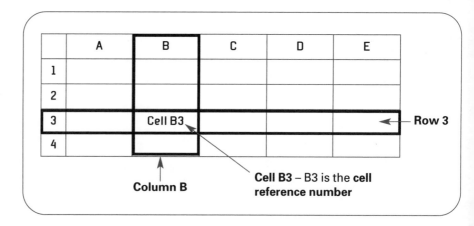

In figure 3.1 the cell pointer is in column B and row 3. Therefore, this cell is referred to as **B3** (cell reference). Into each cell you can type a number, a label or a formula.

Number: This is any number on which a calculation can be made.

Label: This is normally text used for headings e.g. Monday, Tuesday and Wednesday etc. but can also include numbers and symbols that are not used for calculation purposes.

Formula: These will perform calculations for you automatically.

The great thing about a spreadsheet is that once you have entered formulae, you can change the contents of other cells and the answers should still be right.

The computer screen shows only part of the complete spreadsheet, if you scroll down you will see it contains thousands of rows and if you scroll across you will see it has hundreds of columns. Some spreadsheet packages have more than one worksheet.

Using a Formula

Formulae are entered using cell references and not the actual numbers in the cells. When a formula is typed into a cell, the result of the calculation is displayed in the cell, not the formula.

A simple formula can be used to add, subtract, multiply or divide numbers. To carry out these sorts of calculations the following mathematical symbols are used in a formula:

+ (add)

– (subtract)

* (multiply)

/ (divide)

() (brackets are used whenever necessary)

Suppose, for example, that you wanted to add two numbers on a spreadsheet together. If the numbers were in cells **A1** and **A2** the formula that you would need to enter would be something like this:

=A1+A2

You would need to enter this formula in the cell where you wanted the answer to appear.

The '=' sign at the beginning of the formula is there to tell the spreadsheet package that what's been entered is a formula. Some spreadsheet packages use a different symbol to do this.

Functions

To make it easier to enter a longer, more complicated formula, spreadsheet packages also have special **mathematical functions** built-in. Two of the most commonly used functions are used to calculate either the **SUM** or **AVERAGE** of a range of cells. Suppose, for example, that you had a formula like this:

=A1+A2+A3+A4+A5+A6+A7

This formula would add up all the numbers in cells **A1** to **A7**. Instead of typing in such a long formula, the **SUM** function could be used. On most spreadsheets the formula would be something like this:

=SUM(A1:A7)

If a number of cells need the same formula it can be copied and pasted in the same way as text.

Similarly, to work out the average of numbers in cells **A1** to **A7**, the **AVERAGE** function could be used. On most spreadsheets the formula would be something like this:

=AVERAGE(A1:A7)

Exactly what you need to type in will depend upon the spreadsheet package that you are using.

Other mathematical functions

We have already looked at two of the most commonly used mathematical functions: SUM and AVERAGE. Other mathematical functions that you may use are **MAXIMUM, MINIMUM, IF** and **LOOKUP**.

To work out the maximum of numbers in cells **A1** to **A7** the **MAXIMUM** function could be used. On most spreadsheets the formula would be something like this:

=MAXIMUM(A1:A7)

Similarly to work out the minimum of numbers in cells **A1** to **A7** the **MINIMUM** function could be used. On most spreadsheets the formula would be something like this:

=MINIMUM(A1:A7)

An **IF** function is a special type of function that can make a decision based on information supplied to it by the spreadsheet user. Each IF function consists of a condition, a true action and a false action, for example in figure 3.2 a teacher is going to use the

IF function to determine whether a student passed or failed.

Figure 3.2

	A	B	C	D	E	F	G
1				1Blue			
2	Surname	Name	Xmas	Easter	Summer	Average Mark	Pass/Fail
3	King	Andy	45	50	55	50	
4	Daly	Eric	58	62	65	62	
5	Walsh	David	35	38	45	39	
6	Casey	Joe	79	82	85	82	
7	Foye	Kerry	45	49	54	49	
8	Ellis	Jade	43	50	55	49	
9							
10	Pass Mark	60					

If a student's average mark is equal to, or greater than, the pass
mark the teacher wants the spreadsheet to write 'PASS' beside
their name, otherwise it should write 'FAIL'. On most
spreadsheets the formula would be something like this:

=IF(F3=>60,PASS, FAIL)

This formula would be entered in cell G3 and then be copied to
the other cells.

The **LOOKUP** function is a special type of function that can look
up a code or value and insert the relevant value associated with
the code. For example, in figure 3.3 the LOOKUP function is going
to be used to calculate the receipts for each category:

Figure 3.3

	A	B	C
1		Leadmore Swimming Pool	
2	Category	Weekday Mon–Thurs	
3	Adult	€6.00	
4	Child U12	€2.00	
5			
6	Attendance	Mon–Thurs	Receipts
7	Adult	35	
8	Child U12	35	

The range A3 to B4 is called the lookup table, where the program looks for information. You can insert a formula in cell C7 to calculate the amount of receipts for adults by using a lookup function. On most spreadsheets the formula would look something like this:

=LOOKUP(A7,$A$3:$B$4)*B7

The lookup range is referred to using absolute cell references, which means it can be copied.

Exactly what you need to type in will depend upon the spreadsheet package that you are using.

Absolute and Relative Referencing

By default most spreadsheet programs use **relative referencing** in formulae. This means that when a formula is moved or copied to other cells the cell reference changes to that of the new cell. Sometimes you don't want the cell reference to change when you copy a formula and then you need to use an **absolute reference**. Cell references can be made absolute by typing **$** on either side of the column letter.

Examples of Relative and Absolute Cell References

Relative	Absolute
B3	$B$3
A20	$A$20
C15	$C$15

Spreadsheet Features

All spreadsheet packages have many special features in common these include:

Cell Formats

Spreadsheet packages have built-in formatting options, which allow you to change the way a spreadsheet looks. Anything that affects the appearance of a cell is called a **cell format**. Some of the more commonly used **cell formatting** options include:

Changing Font Size and Style

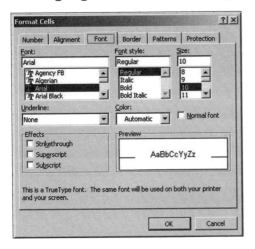

The size and style of text in individual cells or groups of cells can be changed. Different styles of texts are called fonts. In most spreadsheet packages **bold**, *italic*, <u>underlined</u> and different coloured text can all be used.

Figure 3.4: Changing font style and size

Text Alignment

The position of text in a cell is known as **text alignment**. This can be changed easily using text alignment formats. Text can be aligned **vertically** (up and down) or **horizontally** (flat). **Justification** is a type of horizontal alignment. The contents of a cell can be justified **left**, **right**, or in the **centre**.

Figure 3.5: Changing the alignment of text

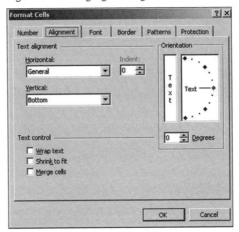

Borders and Lines

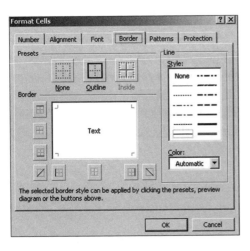

Individual cells or groups of cells can have borders drawn around them. In most spreadsheet packages the style, thickness and colour of the line can be changed.

Figure 3.6: Putting a border around cells

Inserting Rows and Columns

At times, when working with a spreadsheet, it becomes necessary to insert an extra row or an extra column. Most spreadsheets allow you to do this without too much difficulty. When an extra row or column is inserted the spreadsheet should automatically update the cell references in any formulae that are affected by the change.

Changing Column Width and Row Height

The size of a cell depends upon two things:
- The width of the column in which the cell is located.
- The height of the row in which the cell is located.

When any spreadsheet is being set up for the first time all the columns and rows have the same height and width, which means that all the cells are the same size. At this stage the size of the cell is said to be set to the **default value**.

When data is entered into a cell it might not fit into the size allowed by the default value. If this is the case, you can adjust the column width until the data fits in the cell. Similarly, if a row is too low (or too high), its height can be changed. Some spreadsheets can be set up to automatically adjust the column width when data is entered. This option is often called '**best-fit**' or '**auto-size**'.

Figure 3.7: Changing row height

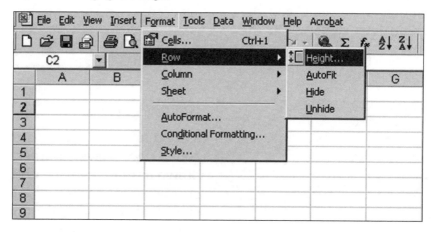

Data Formats

Anything that affects the appearance of numbers in a cell is called **data format**. Some of the more commonly used data format options include:

Decimal

Decimal data format is used when a number needs a decimal point. When using decimal format you have to select the required number of decimal places. For example, to display two decimal places after the decimal point the data format would be '**0.00**' or '**#.##**' depending upon the particular spreadsheet package that is being used.

Currency

A lot of spreadsheets are used for financial calculations. Currency format is used to display the €, or sometimes the $, symbol in front of a number. The required number of decimal places (normally 2 or 0) can be specified in the currency format.

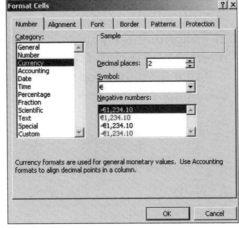

Figure 3.8: Specifying a currency format of 2 decimal places

Date

Date format is used in cells where dates have been entered to specify the way that the date should be displayed. For example, a date format of **dd-mm-yy**, would display the date **12th January 2005** as **12-01-05**; while a format of **dd-mmm-yyy**, would display the same date as **12-Jan-2005**.

Sorting Data

The sort facility in a spreadsheet allows the columns or rows of a spreadsheet to be sorted into **alphabetical** or **numerical** order of a value, in a particular row or column.

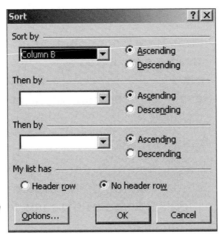

Figure 3.9: Data can be sorted quickly on a spreadsheet

Graphs and Charts

Nearly all spreadsheet packages have the ability to represent information in the form of a graph or chart. The more common types of charts and graphs that are used are **bar charts**, **pie charts** and **line graphs**.

2. Spreadsheet Assignments 1–25

Assignment 1

In assignment 1 you will: •**Enter data** •**Change column width** •**Format text (bold)** •**Enter formula (addition)** •**Save.**

Table 3.1 shows book sales for the months of November and December at The Book Store.

 Note

You can change the width of **column A** so that the words 'The Book Store' fit into cell A1.

Table 3.1

	A	B	C	D
1	The Book Store			
2	Title	November	December	Total Sold
3	House Plant Expert	10	34	
4	Gardens by Design	16	44	
5	Gardening Year	8	27	
6	Herb Gardens	25	45	

Task 1
Key in the information shown in table 3.1.
Task 2
Change the column headings to **bold** format.
Task 3
In the **Total Sold** column enter the formula to calculate the total sales for each book.
Task 4
Save the spreadsheet as **GARDEN**.

 Tip

ALWAYS check the results of formulae to make sure the answers are reasonable – because it is easy to make an error when entering formulae.

Assignment 2

In assignment 2 you will: •Enter data •Change column width •Format text (bold) •**Enter formulae (SUM function)** •Save.

Table 3.2 shows CD sales for the months January to March at The Music Store.

Task 1

Key in the information shown in table 3.2.

Task 2

Change the column headings to **bold** format.

Task 3

In the **Total Sales** column enter the formula to calculate the total sales for each CD.

Task 4

In the **Monthly Sales** row enter the formula to calculate how many CDs were sold each month.

Task 5

Save the spreadsheet as **MUSIC**.

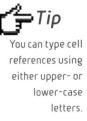

Tip

You can type cell references using either upper- or lower-case letters.

Table 3.2

	A	B	C	D	E
1	The Music Store				
2	CD	Jan	Feb	March	Total Sales
3	Clubmix I	10	14	12	
4	Clubmix II	6	18	19	
5	Club Anthems	8	19	15	
6	Miniistry Mix I	25	82	8	
7	Rock Hits	24	16	29	
8	Monthly Sales				

Assignment 3

In assignment 3 you will: •Enter data •Change column width •Format text (bold) **•Justify text (centre)** •Enter formulae (SUM function) •Save **•Print**.

Table 3.3 shows the results of a year group survey on the number of students who watched *Eastenders* in January.

Table 3.3

	A	B	C	D	E	F
1	Programme	Week 1	Week 2	Week 3	Week 4	Total Viewers
2	Eastenders (Mon)	23	0	16	19	
3	Eastenders (Tue)	20	17	19	13	
4	Eastenders (Thurs)	14	18	10	13	
5	Eastenders (Fri)	0	9	11	17	
6	Weekly Total					

Task 1
Key in the information shown in table 3.3.
Task 2
Centre the column headings and change their format to **bold**.
Task 3
In the **Total Viewers** column enter the formula to calculate the total viewers of each programme.
Task 4
In the **Weekly Total** row enter formula to calculate the total number of viewers for each week.
Task 5
Save the spreadsheet as **TV**.
Task 6
Print one copy of the spreadsheet with your name on it.

Assignment 4
In assignment 4 you will: •Enter data •Change column width •Format text (bold and italics) •Justify text (centre) •**Format data (currency)** •Enter Formula (**Subtraction**) •Save •Print.

The Book Store is having a sale on travel books. Table 3.4 shows the pre-sale price of some books and the discount available.

Table 3.4

	A	B	C	D
1	The Book Store			
2	Title	Price	Discount	Sales Price
3	Ibiza Uncovered	€15.99	€2.00	
4	Majorca Uncovered	€15.99	€2.00	
5	Southern Spain	€17.99	€2.50	
6	Rhodes Pocket Guide	€13.99	€1.00	
7	Portugal Uncovered	€15.99	€2.00	
8	Tuscan Treasures	€18.99	€3.00	

Task 1
Key in the information shown in table 3.4.
Task 2
Centre the column headings and change their format to bold and italics.

Task 3

In the **Sale Price** column enter the formula to calculate the sale price for each book. (Subtract discount from price.)

Task 4

Save the spreadsheet as **TRAVEL** and print one copy.

Assignment 5

In assignment 5 you will: •Enter data •Change column width •Format text (bold and italics) •Justify text (centre) •Enter formulae (SUM and **AVERAGE function**) •**Insert new row** •Save •Print.

Table 3.5 shows the music magazine sales at Noel's Newsagents from July to September.

Table 3.5

	A	B	C	D	E
1	Magazine	July	August	Sept	Total Sales
2	Smash Hits	63	75	60	
3	Metalworks	29	22	26	
4	Q	56	59	62	
5	Rolling Stone	43	40	49	
6	Hot Press	18	21	26	
7	Average Monthly Sales				

Task 1

Key in the information shown in table 3.5.

Task 2

Centre the column headings and change their format to bold and italics.

Task 3

In the **Total Sales** column enter the formula to calculate the total sales for each magazine.

Task 4

In the **Average Monthly Sales** row enter the formula to calculate the **AVERAGE** sales for each month.

Task 5

Insert a new row at the top of the spreadsheet and enter the name of the shop **Noel's Newsagents**.

Task 6

Save the spreadsheet as **NEWS** and print one copy with your name on it.

 Tip

You can 'point' at a cell to include it in a formula instead of typing the reference.

Assignment 6

In assignment 6 you will: •Enter data •Change column width •Format text (bold and colour) •Format data (currency) •Enter formula (SUM function and **multiplication**) •Save •Print.

Table 3.6 shows the sales in the school shop for the first week of March.

Table 3.6

	A	B	C	D	E	F	G	H	I
1	School Shop								
2	Item	Mon	Tues	Wed	Thurs	Fri	Total Sold	Price	Income
3	Tayto	63	56	49	55	45		€0.50	
4	Cereal Bar	29	32	42	23	63		€0.60	
5	Snickers	18	22	18	29	25		€0.70	
6	Twix	56	46	49	45	45		€0.75	
7	Coke-Can	129	63	56	56	78		€0.80	
8	Fanta-Can	36	28	23	62	69		€0.80	

Task 1
Enter the data as shown in table 3.6.
Task 2
Apply bold formatting to the column headings and change the colour of the text to blue.
Task 3
In the **Total Sold** column enter the formula to calculate the total number sold for each item.
Task 4
In the **Income** column enter the formula to show the income for each item. (Price multiplied by Total Sold.)
Task 5
Save the spreadsheet as **SHOP** and print one copy with your name on it.

Assignment 7

In assignment 7 you will: •**Open existing file** •Enter new data •Currency format •**Copy and paste formulae** •Save •Print.

Task 1
Open the spreadsheet called **SHOP**. (Assignment 6)

Task 2
Some of the information was left out of the spreadsheet, please enter the data shown in table 3.7.

Table 3.7

	A	B	C	D	E	F	G	H	I
1	Item	Mon	Tue	Wed	Thurs	Fri	Total Sold	Price	Income
9	Onion Rings	12	16	22	13	23		€0.50	
10	Skips	42	46	10	46	53		€0.50	
11	Crunchie	19	26	13	55	45		€0.80	
12	Animal Bar	29	18	42	48	12		€0.30	

Task 3
Use the copy and paste command to enter the formula in the **Total Sold** column to calculate the total number sold for each item.

Task 4
Use the copy and paste command to enter the formula in the **Income** column to show the income for each item.

Task 5
Save the spreadsheet as **SHOP1** and print one copy with your name on it.

Tip

You can copy formulae using the Fill handle too.

Assignment 8

In assignment 8 you will: •Enter data •Change column width •Format text (bold, italics and colour) •Justify text (centre) •Enter formulae (Average, **Minimum and Maximum function**) •Copy and paste formula •Insert new row •Save •Print.

Table 3.8 shows a section of a spreadsheet that holds test results for a class at Leadmore Community College.

Table 3.8

	A	B	C	D	E	F
1	Surname	Name	Xmas	Easter	Summer	Average Result
2	Smith	Joe	67	85	58	
3	Jones	Adam	80	80	78	
4	Kelly	Tom	60	70	72	
5	Court	Jack	59	65	70	
6	Collins	Mick	58	83	79	
7	Barry	John	83	87	92	
8	Maximum Mark					
9	Minimum Mark					

Task 1
Key in the information shown in table 3.8.

Task 2
Centre the column headings, change their format to bold and italics and change the colour of the text to red.

Task 3
In the **Average Result** column enter the formula to calculate the average result for each student. Use copy and paste to enter this formula in the remaining cells.

Task 4
In the **Maximum Mark** row enter the formula to calculate the maximum mark for each test i.e. Xmas, Easter and Summer.

Task 5
In the **Minimum Mark** row enter the formula to calculate the minimum mark for each test.

Task 6
Insert a new row at the top of the spreadsheet and enter the name of the class **1Red**.

Task 7
Save the spreadsheet as **RESULTS** and print one copy with your name on it.

Assignment 9

In assignment 9 you will: •Open an existing file •**Change data** •Enter new data •Change column width •**Insert new columns** •Format data (currency) •Enter formulae (multiplication and subtraction) •Save •Print.

Task 1

Open the spreadsheet called **MUSIC**. (Assignment 2)

Task 2

A mistake was made when adding the numbers for the CD **Clubmix I**. Change the data for this CD to that shown in table 3.9.

Table 3.9

2	CD	Jan	Feb	March	Total Sales
3	Clubmix I	20	16	22	

Task 3

Add a new column called **Price** after the **Total Sales** column and enter the price for each CD as shown in table 3.10.

Task 4

The Music Store is having a sale; there is 10% off all CDs. Add a new column after the **Price** column called **Discount** and enter the formula to calculate how much the discount will be on each CD. (Multiply the Price by 10%.)

Table 3.10

	A	F
1	CD	Price
2	Clubmix I	€19.99
3	Clubmix II	€20.99
4	Club Anthems	€19.99
5	Ministry Mix I	€21.99
6	Rock Hits	€20.99

Task 5

Add a new column after the **Discount** column called **Sale Price** and enter the formula to calculate the Sale Price of each CD. (Subtract the Discount from the Price.)

Task 6

Save the spreadsheet as **SALE** and print one copy with your name and today's date on it.

Assignment 10

In assignment 10 you will: •Enter data •Change column width •Insert new column and rows •Use average, maximum and minimum functions •**Sort data** •Save •Print.

Table 3.11 shows the temperature at 14:00 hrs over five days in August (15–19th) at six locations throughout the country.

Table 3.11

	A	B	C	D	E	F
1	Temperature	Record	(°C)			
2	Location	Monday	Tuesday	Wednesday	Thursday	Friday
3	Newbridge	22	23	26	25	27
4	Castlebar	23	21	25	25	26
5	Ennis	24	22	26	27	26
6	Thurles	23	24	27	26	23
7	Cork	20	21	28	25	24
8	Athlone	22	20	24	25	24

Task 1
Key in the information shown in table 3.11.

Task 2
Add a new column called **Average** and use the average function to find the average temperature at each location over the five days.

Task 3
Add a new row called **Maximum** and use the maximum function to calculate the overall maximum daily temperature.

Task 4
Add a new row called **Minimum** and use the minimum function to calculate the overall minimum daily temperature.

Task 5
Sort the data in alphabetical order.

Task 6
Save the spreadsheet as **TEMP** and print one copy with your name and today's date on it.

Assignment 11

In assignment 11 you will: •Enter data •Change column width •Format text (bold) •Justify text (centre) •Format data (number and decimal place) •Use SUM function •**Draw chart** •Save •Print.

Table 3.12 shows the sales figures for Esker Motors between April and June.

Table 3.12

	A	B	C	D	E
1	Esker Motors				
2	Car	April	May	June	Total Sold
3	Corsa	12	10	6	
4	Astra	15	12	11	
5	Vectra	9	5	7	
6	Meriva	6	3	8	
7	Zafira	2	5	6	

Task 1
Key in the information shown in table 3.12.

Task 2
In the **Total Sold** column insert the formula to calculate the total number sold for each type of car.

Task 3
Centre the column headings and change their format to bold.

Task 4
Sort the data in alphabetical order.

Task 5
With the information you have in the **Car** and **Total Sold** columns, draw a bar chart to show the data.

Task 6
Save the spreadsheet as **ESKER** and print one copy of the spreadsheet and the chart with your name and today's date on it.

 Note

The Y-axis is the vertical line on the left of the chart. The X-axis is the horizontal line at the bottom of the chart.

Assignment 12

In assignment 12 you will: •Enter data •Change column width •**Change font size** and style •Justify text (centre) •Format data (number and decimal place) •Use average function •Draw chart •Save •Print.

Table 3.13 shows the number of homes in and around Leadmore to which a free newspaper the Leadmore Times was delivered between July and December.

Table 3.13

	A	B	C	D	E	F	G	H
1	Location	July	August	Sept	Oct	Nov	Dec	Average
2	Leadmore	300	350	350	350	400	400	
3	Ballybay	200	200	250	250	250	250	
4	Avondale	100	100	150	150	150	170	
5	Esker	50	50	55	55	60	60	
6	Deryvale	170	170	200	200	205	205	

Task 1
Key in the information shown in table 3.13.
Task 2
In the **Average** column enter the formula to calculate the average number of homes in each area, to which the paper was delivered over the six months.
Task 3
Format the numbers in the **Average** column as number values to zero decimal places.
Task 4
Centre the column headings, change their format to bold and change the font size of the whole spreadsheet to size 8.
Task 5
Sort the data in alphabetical order.
Task 6
With the information you have in the **Location** and **Average** columns, draw a bar chart to show the data.
Task 7
Save the spreadsheet as **TIMES** and print one copy with your name and today's date on it.

Tip
You may need to reduce the font size on the X- or Y-axis to see all the data.

Assignment 13

In assignment 13 you will: •Open an existing file •Enter new data •**Insert new columns** •Change column width •Format data (number and zero decimal place) •Copy and paste formulae •Draw chart •Save •Print.

Task 1
Open the spreadsheet called **TEMP**. (Assignment 10)

Task 2
Add two new columns for Saturday and Sunday between the **Friday** and the **Average** columns and insert the data in table 3.14.

Task 3
Format the numbers in the **Average** column as number values to one decimal place.

Task 4
Use the copy and paste facility to find the maximum and minimum daily temperatures in the two new columns.

Table 3.14

	A	G	H
2	Location	Saturday	Sunday
3	Athlone	21	20
4	Castlebar	23	20
5	Cork	21	20
6	Ennis	24	21
7	Newbridge	22	20
8	Thurles	23	22

Tip

If a number changes to #### when you format a cell this means you need to increase the column width.

Note

Check the formulae in the Average column – to make sure the new data is included in the answer!

Task 5
Change the font size of the whole spreadsheet to size 8.

Task 6
With the information you have in the **Location** and **Average** columns, draw a bar chart to show the data.

Task 7
Save the spreadsheet as **TEMP1** and print one copy with your name and today's date on it.

Assignment 14

In assignment 14 you will: •Open an existing file •Insert new column •Change column width •Enter formulae (average function) •Draw chart •Save •Print (**landscape orientation**).

Task 1
Open the spreadsheet called **SHOP1**. (Assignment 7)

Task 2
Insert a new column called **Average Number Sold** between the **Total Sold** and the **Price** column and use the average function to calculate the average number sold of each item.

Task 3

Add a new column called **Percentage Sales** between the **Average Number Sold** and the **Price** column and insert the formula to calculate the percentage sales of each item (as a percentage of the total sold).

Task 4

Change the font size of the whole spreadsheet to size 8.

Task 5

With the information you have in the **Item** and **Percentage Sales** columns, draw a pie chart to show the data.

Task 6

Format the pie so that you will see the item name and percentage sales on each piece.

Task 7

Save the spreadsheet as **SHOP2** and print one copy in landscape orientation with your name and today's date on it.

Tip

Landscape orientation means the page is printed sideways. With Portrait orientation the page is printed lengthways like a page in this book.

Assignment 15

In assignment 15 you will: •Enter data •Change column width •Format data (currency) •Insert new row •**Enter formulae using absolute cell addresses** •Sort data •Save •Print.

The spreadsheet shown in table 3.15 is used in Tracy's Travel Lodge to calculate the bill for each customer.

Table 3.15

	A	B	C	D	E	F
1	Service	Charge	10%			
2	Surname	Price P/N	No. Nights	Subtotal	Service Charge	Total
3	Smith	€40.00	4			
4	Murphy	€35.00	6			
5	Callaghan	€35.00	9			
6	Butler	€40.00	5			
7	Kenny	€35.00	9			
8	Adams	€35.00	6			
9	Canning	€35.00	14			

Task 1

Key in the information shown in table 3.15.

Task 2

Add a new row between the row for **Callaghan** and the row for **Butler** and enter the data in table 3.16.

Table 3.16

Surname	Price P/N	No, Nights	Subtotal	Service Charge	Total
Flanagan	€35.00	12			

Task 3
In the **Subtotal** column enter the formula to work out the subtotal for each guest. (Price P/N multiplied by No. Nights.)

Task 4
In the **Service Charge** column enter the formula using an absolute cell address to work out the service charge each guest has to pay.

Task 5
In the **Total** column enter formula to work out the total bill for each guest. (Subtotal plus Service Charge.)

Task 6
Sort the data in ascending order.

Task 7
Insert a new row at the top of the spreadsheet and enter the heading **Tracy's Travel Lodge.**

Task 8
Save the spreadsheet as **LODGE** and print one copy with your name and today's date on it.

Tip

When you copy or move a formula containing an absolute cell reference, the cell reference does not change.

Assignment 16
In assignment 16 you will: •Enter data •**Merge cells** •Change data •Change column width •Insert new column and row •Format data (**date** and currency) •Enter formula (multiplication, division and SUM function) •Use absolute cell references •Sort data •Save •Print (landscape orientation).

Table 3.17 shows the bookings at Football Trips Ltd for the month of November.

Table 3.17

	A	B	C	D	E	F	G	H
1				Football Trips Ltd				
2	Commission	1%						
3	Team	Code	Destination	Cost	No. Nights	Numbers	Income	Commission
4	Man. United	MU01	London	€399.00	1	77		
5	Man. United	MU03	Barcelona	€599.00	2	59		
6	Arsenal	AR02	Amsterdam	€499.00	2	93		
7	Chelsea	CH01	London	€389.00	1	67		
8	Leeds Utd	LU01	Leeds	€349.00	1	42		
9	Liverpool	LP01	Liverpool	€399.00	1	88		
10	AC Milan	AC01	Milan	€559.00	2	36		

Task 1

Key in the information shown in table 3.17.

Task 2

Change the numbers for code MU03 to 67 and AC01 to 43.

Task 3

The cost of trip LU01 has increased to €399.00.

Task 4

Insert a new column called **Date** between the **Destination** and **Cost** columns and insert the data in table 3.18.

Task 5

In the **Income** column enter the formula to calculate the Total Income from each trip. (Cost multiplied by numbers.)

Task 6

Add a new row called **Monthly Income** and enter the formula to calculate the income for the month.

Task 7

Travel consultants at Football Trips Ltd earn 1% commission on each trip sold. In the **Commission** column enter the formula, using absolute cell references, to calculate how much commission was earned on each trip.

Task 8

The commission is divided equally each month between three staff members. Add new rows to calculate (a) Total Commission and (b) Amount per Person.

Task 9

Save the spreadsheet as **FOOTBALL** and print one copy in landscape orientation with your name and today's date on it.

Table 3.18

Code	Date
MU01	09/11
MU03	16/11
AR02	19/11
CH01	01/11
LU01	19/11
LP01	24/11
AC01	24/11

Assignment 17

In Assignment 17 you will: •Enter data •Merge cells •Change column width •Enter formula (AVERAGE and IF functions) •Save •Print.

Table 3.19 (on next page) shows a record of student's exam results over the course of a year.

Task 1

Create the spreadsheet as shown in table 3.19.

Task 2

In the **Average Mark** column insert the formula to calculate the average mark for each student.

Table 3.19

	A	B	C	D	E	F	G
1	1 BLUE						
2	Surname	Name	Xmas	Easter	Summer	Average Mark	Pass/Fail
3	King	Andy	45	50	55		
4	Daly	Eric	58	62	65		
5	Walsh	David	35	38	45		
6	Casey	Joe	79	82	85		
7	Foye	Kerry	45	49	54		
8	Ellis	Jade	43	50	55		
9							
10	Pass Mark	60					

Task 3

In the **Pass/Fail** column insert the formula using the IF function to determine whether students have passed or failed.

If a student's average mark is equal to or greater than the pass mark, you want the spreadsheet to write 'PASS' beside their name, otherwise it should write 'FAIL'.

Task 4

Save the spreadsheet as **MARK** and print one copy.

Assignment 18

In assignment 18 you will: •Enter data •Merge cells •Change column width •Enter formula (SUM and IF functions) •Save •Print.

Table 3.20 shows the number of books sold by each sales assistant in The Book Store between April and June.

Table 3.20

	A	B	C	D	E	F	G
1	The Book Store						
2	Commission	€0.25					
3	Name	April	May	June	Total Sold	Bonus	Amount
4	Janet	56	45	60			
5	Mary	63	56	59			
6	David	45	44	50			
7	Keith	59	50	45			
8	Dan	57	65	48			
9							
10	Bonus Number	150					

Task 1

Create the spreadsheet as shown in table 3.20.

Task 2

In the **Total Sold** column insert the formula to calculate the total sales for each assistant.

Task 3

In the **Bonus** column insert the formula, using the IF function, to determine whether each assistant qualifies for a bonus or not.

If the total sold by an assistant is equal to or greater than the bonus number, you want the spreadsheet to write 'Yes' beside their name, otherwise it should write 'No'.

Task 4

In the **Amount** column enter the formula, using the IF function and absolute cell references, to determine the amount of commission each qualifying assistant should receive this quarter. Sales assistants receive €0.25 commission for every book they sell.

Task 5

Save the spreadsheet as **BONUS** and print one copy.

Assignment 19

In assignment 19 you will: •Enter data •Merge cells •Change column width •Format data (currency) •Enter formula (SUM and IF functions) •Use absolute cell references •Insert new row •Save •Print.

Table 3.21 shows a spreadsheet used by Mill Hill Insurance to calculate the quarterly commission for each sales person and the bonus due to each one.

Table 3.21

	A	B	C	D	E
1	Mill Hill Insurance				
2	Commission	1.75%			
3	Month	Nolan	Mackey	Davis	Brady
4	January	€399,000	€456,000	€222,000	€423,000
5	February	€256,000	€123,652	€321,080	€125,300
6	March	€236,700	€546,000	€285,600	€563,123
7	Total				

Task 1

Key in the information shown in table 3.21.

Task 2

In the **Total** row enter the formula to calculate the total sales for each sales person.

Task 3

Add a new row called **Quarter Commission** and, using absolute cell references, enter the formulae to calculate the quarterly commission earned by each person.

Task 4

Add a new row called **Bonus** and insert the formula, using the IF function, to calculate whether a bonus is due or not. To qualify for a bonus each person must have earned more than €15,000 in commission. If they qualify for a bonus they get €1,000, otherwise they get nothing (Zero).

Task 5

Save the spreadsheet as **MHILL** and print one copy with your name and today's date on it.

Assignment 20

In assignment 20 you will: •Open existing file •Delete row •Enter new data •Enter formula (SUM and IF+AND functions) •Insert column and row •Save •Print (landscape orientation).

Task 1

Open the spreadsheet called **FOOTBALL**. (Assignment 16)

Task 2

The trip to see Chelsea (code CH01) had to be cancelled at the last minute. Please delete this row from the spreadsheet.

Task 3

Add a new row between Arsenal (code AR02) and Leeds (code LU01) and enter the information in table 3.22.

Table 3.22

Team	Code	Destination	Date	Cost	No. Nights	Numbers
Aston Villa	AV01	Birmingham	19/11	€359.00	2	35

Task 4

Insert a new column called **Bonus** in an appropriate position in the spreadsheet and insert the formula, using the IF function, to calculate whether a bonus is due or not. To qualify for a bonus 50 people or more must travel on each trip and the cost of the trip must be €399.00 or more. If the trip then qualifies for a bonus the agency gets €100.00 otherwise they get nothing.

Task 5

Add a new row called **Total Bonus** after the **Amount per Person** row and enter the formula: (**a**) to calculate the total bonus earned that month, and (**b**) to calculate what bonus each travel consultant earned. (There are 3 staff members.)

Task 6

Add a new row called **Overall Earnings** and enter the formula to calculate how much a travel consultant would earn in bonus and commission that month.

Task 7

Save the spreadsheet as **FOOTIE** and print one copy in landscape orientation with your name and today's date on it.

Assignment 21

In assignment 21 you will: •Open existing file •Enter new data •Change column width •Insert column •Enter formula (IF function) •Draw chart •**Protect spreadsheet** •Save •Print.

Task 1

Open the spreadsheet called **MHILL**. (Assignment 19)

Task 2

A new member of staff called Ryan joined in February, add a new column between the columns for Mackey and Davis and enter the data in table 3.23.

Table 3.23

Month	Ryan
February	€157,010
March	€239,500

Task 3

Enter the formulae to find the following: (**a**) Total, (**b**) Quarter Commission, and (**c**) Bonus, for Ryan.

Task 4

Tip

When choosing a password pick one you will remember easily but which is not too obvious.

With the information you have in the spreadsheet draw a bar chart to show the monthly data for each salesperson.

Task 5

Save the spreadsheet as **MHILL1** and print one copy with your name and today's date on it.

Task 6

This spreadsheet is confidential. Please add a form of protection to the spreadsheet so that it can't be changed by anyone other than those with a specific password.

Assignment 22

In assignment 22 you will: •Enter data •Change column width •Merge cells •Format data (currency) •Enter formula (addition, division, subtraction, IF function) •Use absolute cell references •**Insert picture** •Save •**Print** (landscape) **showing formulae**.

Table 3.24 shows some of the costs associated with running John's Ice Cream Van in July and August.

Table 3.24

	A	B	C	D	E
1		John's Ice Cream Sales			
2					
3	Fixed Costs				
4	Van rental	€1,200			
5	Equipment Hire	€535			
6					
7	Total Fixed Costs				
8					
9	Unit Costs	Ice Cream	Ice Lollies		
10	Cost per box (60)	€15.00	€10.00		
11	Cost per unit				
12	Selling Price	€1.00	€0.80		
13	Profit per unit				
14					
15		Sunny Day	Cloudy Day	Rainy Day	
16	Sales per day				
17	Ice Cream	140	40	10	
18	Lollies	170	25	0	
19	Daily Profit				
20		Sunny Day	Cloudy Day	Rainy Day	Total
21	Number of Days	30	20		
22	Gross Profit				
23	Total fixed costs				
24	Net Profit				
25					

Task 1
Create the spreadsheet shown in table 3.24.

Task 2
Enter the formula to work out the **Total Fixed Costs**.

Task 3

Enter the formulae to work out the **Cost per unit** for ice cream and lollies, assuming there are 60 in each box. (Cost per box divided by 60.)

Tip

Enter a formula, not a value, in cell D21 – there are 62 days in July and August.

Task 4

Enter the formulae to work out the **Profit per unit** for ice cream and lollies. (Cost per unit subtracted from selling price.)

Task 5

Using absolute cell references enter the formula in the **Daily Profit** row to work out the daily profit for sunny, cloudy and rainy days.

Task 6

In the **Gross Profit** row enter the formula to work out the gross profit for: (**a**) each type of day, and (**b**) the total gross profit.

Task 7

Add one example of clipart in an appropriate position to reflect the theme of the spreadsheet.

Task 8

Add a new row called **Viability** and use the IF function to work out whether the job is **Viable** or **Not Viable**. John has decided that if he cannot make a profit of at least €2,000 it wouldn't be viable.

Task 9

Is John's business viable? What if it is a bad summer with few sunny days? Reduce the number of sunny days to 10 and see what happens.

Tip

Removing the Gridlines can sometimes improve the appearance of your spreadsheet.

Task 10

Save the spreadsheet as **ICE** and print one copy with landscape orientation, showing formulae, with your name and today's date on it.

Assignment 23

In assignment 23 you will: •Enter data •Change column width •Merge cells •Increase row height •Wrap text •Format data (currency) •Insert new column and row •Enter formula (addition, SUM and **LOOKUP function**) •Draw chart •Save •Print.

Table 3.25 (on the next page) is used to calculate the receipts at Leadmore swimming pool.

Task 1

Key in the information shown in table 3.25.

Task 2

In the **Receipts** column enter the formula, using the LOOKUP function, to calculate the weekday receipts for each group of people.

Table 3.25

	A	B	C	D	E
1			Leadmore Swimming Pool		
2		Weekday Mon–Thurs	Weekend Fri–Sun		
3	Adult	€6.00	€7.00		
4	Child U12	€2.00	€3.00		
5	OAP	€2.00	€3.00		
6	Student	€3.00	€4.00		
7					
8	Attendance	Mon–Thurs	Receipts	Fri–Sun	Receipts
9	Adult	35		70	
10	Child U12	35		82	
11	OAP	9		6	
12	Student	46		56	

Task 3
Using the LOOKUP function do the same with the **Receipts** column for the weekend.

Task 4
Add a new column called **Total** and enter the formulae to add the receipts for each group.

Task 5
Add a new row called **Weekly Total** and enter the formula to calculate the income for the week.

Task 6
Draw two charts, on separate sheets, to show the attendance data for Mon–Thurs and the data for Fri–Sun.

Task 7
Save the spreadsheet as **LSP** and print one copy with your name and today's date on it.

Assignment 24

In assignment 24 you will: •Enter data •Change column width •Merge cells •Format data (currency) •Enter formula (multiplication, SUM and LOOKUP function) •Save •Print.

Table 3.26 shows a spreadsheet used by K. Walsh Heating and Plumbing to calculate the fees owed by each client.

Table 3.26

	A	B	C	D	E
1	Work	Code	Cost		
2	Callout Charge	CA	€35		
3	Clear Blockage	CB	€45		
4	Ins. Dishwasher	IDW	€60		
5	Ins. Radiator	IR	€55		
6	Ins. Washing Machine	IWM	€60		
7					
8	Client	Code	Charges	VAT @ 21%	TOTAL
9	J Andrews	CB			
10	K Quinn	CB			
11	J Stephens	IDW			
12	F Salmon	IDW			
13	M Cunnane	IWM			

Task 1
Key in the information shown in table 3.26.

Task 2
In the **Charges** column enter the formula, using the LOOKUP function, to calculate the cost for each client. The callout charge must be included in all calculations.

Task 3
In the **VAT** column enter the formula to calculate the VAT amount for each client. (Charges multiplied by 21%.)

Task 4
In the **TOTAL** column enter the formula to calculate the total for each client. (Charges plus VAT.)

Task 5
Add a form of protection to the spreadsheet so that the formulae can't be changed by anyone other than those with a specific password.

Task 6
Save the spreadsheet as **WALSHH&P** and print one copy with your name and today's date on it.

Assignment 25
In assignment 25 you will: •Open existing file •**Copy data between spreadsheets** •**Clear data** •Enter new data •Change column width •Enter formula (average, maximum and minimum functions) •Sort data •Save •Print.

Task 1

Open a new spreadsheet.

Task 2

Open the spreadsheet called **TEMP1** (Assignment 13) and copy all the data from this spreadsheet to the one you opened. (Do not include the chart.)

Task 3

Close **TEMP1**.

Task 4

Change the heading in the new spreadsheet to **Wind Speed (kt)**.

Task 5

Clear the data from the days of the week and then enter the data as set out in table 3.27.

Table 3.27

2	Location	Mon	Tues	Wed	Thurs	Fri	Sat	Sun
3	Athlone	1	3	9	3	2	2	2
4	Castlebar	6	7	10	6	4	3	4
5	Cork	3	3	12	8	5	4	4
6	Ennis	5	6	11	5	3	2	3
7	Newbridge	4	5	7	4	2	1	1
8	Thurles	4	5	9	6	3	3	3

Task 6

Save the new spreadsheet as **WIND** and print one copy.

1. Introduction to Databases

Databases are used to store large amounts of information, and allow you to sort and filter the data quickly to provide lists and reports. Databases are found in all sorts of situations that we encounter in our daily lives, from booking a holiday or cinema ticket to registering as a school pupil or library member.

Planning a Database

Databases are complex applications and it is very important to plan the database before entering the information into a computer. It will save time later if your original design satisfies all the user requirements of the database rather than trying to make changes at a later date. When planning a database you need to think about:

- What is the purpose of the database?
- What information will you want to look up in the database?
- What data will you store in the database?

Database Structure

A database is based on tables of data with each table containing many records (rows) and each record is made up of many fields (columns):

- Records contain related information e.g. a person's name, address and telephone number.
- Fields contain only one type of information e.g. dates of birth.

Table 4.1 shows part of a database used by a school to store information about the pupils.

These are the fields – there are four fields in this database

This is one complete record – there are five records in this database

Surname	First Name	Class	Telephone
Jones	Jenny	1Red	056123623
Kenny	Sharon	1Red	056321456
Neary	Mark	1Red	056456123
Carolan	Oisin	1Red	056457896
Dolan	Pat	1Red	056654897

Table 4.1: Records and fields in a database

Data Types

Before you can enter fields into a database, you need to think about what format the data will be in. There are many different types of data:

Table 4.2: Types of data

Text	Letters, symbols and numbers i.e. alphanumeric data.
Number	Numbers only (no letters). Includes numbers with decimal places.
Date/Time	Dates and times.
Currency	For all monetary data.
Logical	Yes/No and True/False answers etc.

Field Length

The length of a field determines how much information can be typed into it. Each character counts as one, e.g. the name Jenny is five characters long. Spaces also count as one character. Field length applies only to text fields and it is important to remember if you choose to set a field length that you account for data that may be entered in the future.

Data Validation

It is important to make sure that you enter the correct data into a database. If you make a mistake entering data, especially in very large databases, the error can be very difficult to trace. In some database packages you can write a set of rules by which the data must abide. The process of checking that the data meets various rules is called validation. If you entered a validation rule in a date of birth field for students born between 01/01/1994 and 31/12/2004 it might look like this:

Between 01/01/1994 And 31/12/2004

This means that the computer will only accept dates of birth between those dates. If you try to enter a date of birth that falls outside those dates a message should appear on the screen containing the validation text that you entered thus reminding you that the data is invalid.

Data Entry Forms

Forms allow you to type data into a database using a specifically designed form rather than straight into a table. They show all the information for one record at a time and provide an easy way of entering data. Forms can also be tailored to accept only certain information, or only information in the correct format and can be formatted using colours, fonts and graphics, which can make them more attractive and easy to use.

Database Features

All database packages have many special features in common, these include:

Searching

Searching a file involves looking for an individual record or group of records that match a certain condition. Searches are also known as **queries**. To search a database you must enter a query. The query tells the software which fields to look at in each record and what to look for. Some of the most commonly used types of queries are set out in Table 4.3.

Table 4.3: Most commonly used types of queries

Operator	Meaning	Example
=	equal to	=20 Will find all records where data in a field is exactly equal to 20.
>=	greater than or equal to	>=20 Will find all records where data in a field is greater than or equal to 20.
<=	less than or equal to	<=20 Will find all records where data in a field is less than 20.
<	less than	<20 Will find all records where data in a field is less than 20.
>	greater than	>20 Will find all records where data in a field is greater than 20.
<>	not equal to	<>20 Will find all records where data in a field does not contain the number 20.
Between	Test for a range of values. Must be two comparison values separated by AND operator.	BETWEEN 20 AND 30 Will find all records where data in a field is between 20 and 30.
And	Test for two or more search criteria.	>=20 AND <=30 Will find all records where data in a field is greater than or equal to the value 20 AND less than or equal to the value 30.
Or	Test for a choice of different search criteria.	=20 OR =30 Will find all the records where data in a field is either equal to 20 or equal to 30.

Some software packages use words instead of symbols in queries, so exactly what you need to type will depend on the software package that you are using.

Wildcard Queries

When making a query, you can use a **wildcard** symbol that will find variations of numbers and text. The asterisk (*) is the most commonly used symbol for wildcard searches. The wildcard symbol is used to indicate the part of the text or number that you are unsure of and is combined with a piece of information to create a search. For example, in a school to find all students whose surname begins with 'K' you would enter 'K*' in the criteria.

Sorting

Sorting involves putting the records in a file into a particular order e.g. alphabetical or numerical order. In a school, for example, a list of all the students in a particular class might need to be printed off in alphabetical order.

The field on which a database is sorted is called the **key field**. Since a database or query can be sorted on more than one field the first field to be sorted is called the **primary key field** and the second field to be sorted is called the **secondary key field**.

Indexing

Another way of sorting a database is to create an index. Using an index in a database makes it faster to find and sort records, especially in large databases. To set up an index you mark a field as indexed. Then, when a new record is added to a database, the index is automatically updated and the record is inserted in the correct position.

Making Calculations

Many common mathematical functions can be used in databases. Numerical (no text) and currency fields can be added together, multiplied, divided or subtracted from each other. Common statistical functions such as average, mean and total can also be used.

Updating

The information stored in a database must be updated regularly or it will cause problems for the business or organisation that is using it. This involves **inserting** new records, **deleting** records that are no longer needed and **amending** the information in a record if it changes. As well as inserting, deleting and amending records it is also possible to insert, delete and amend fields in a database.

Find/Replace
This allows you to find and replace text or numbers quickly in a field or in the complete database.

Reports
This facility allows you to present data in a wide variety of ways and can be based on queries or on tables.

Labels (Mailing etc.)
Address and product labels etc. can be produced from the information held in the database. Most database packages have label wizards to make the task easier.

Merging
Merging means combining two files to produce a new one. This can be done by merging a file containing new records with an existing file, provided that both contain the same set of fields.

2. Database Assignments 1–26

Assignment 1
In Assignment 1 you will: •**Enter field name** •**Select data type** •**Enter data** •**Save**.

Table 4.4 shows information on some of the students who are travelling to the Leadmore Adventure Centre.

Note

If you are using Microsoft Access you will have to name the database at the start.

Table 4.4

Surname	First Name	Telephone	Amount Paid
Judd	Rebecca	4561897	€55.00
Smart	Keith	6781543	€40.00
Murphy	Jack	2347896	€45.00
Dunne	Aoife	2347896	€50.00
Niland	Joe	3475853	€55.00
Cullen	Katie	4467889	€55.00

Task 1
Look at Table 4.4 and answer the following questions:
- How many **records** are there in the database?
- How many **fields** are there in the database?
- What data types are the entries in the **Surname** and **First Name** columns?
- What data types are the entries in the **Telephone** column?
- What data types are the entries in the **Amount Paid** column?

Task 2
Create a suitable database structure for the information given in table 4.4. Use the column headings as the field names and set the appropriate data type.

Task 3
Enter the data shown in table 4.4.

Task 4
Save the database as **LEADMORE**.

Tip
There is no need to type the € sign once the data type of the **Amount Paid** field is set to currency.

Note
MS Access users can use the same file name for the table but prefix it with **TBL** – so the table name will be TBLLEADMORE.

Assignment 2
In Assignment 2 you will: •Enter field name •Select data type •Enter data •Save •**Insert new records**.

Table 4.5 shows information on the teams taking part in a Soccer Blitz.

Table 4.5

Team	Contact Name	Telephone	Paid
Blue Bombers	John	6264934	Yes
Red Devils	Eamonn	2644394	No
White Stripes	Derek	4436942	Yes
Green Arrows	Kevin	7934241	Yes
Silver Linings	Brendan	2649434	No
Pink Panthers	Jackie	7931824	Yes

Task 1
Look at Table 4.5 and answer the following questions:
- How many **records** are there in the database?
- How many **fields** are there in the database?
- What data types are the entries in the **Team** and **Contact Name** columns?

- What data types are the entries in the **Telephone** column?
- What data types are the entries in the **Paid** column?

Tip

Remember that the fields are the column headings.

Note

Using MS Access? If you are – save the table as TBLBLITZ.

Task 2
Create a suitable database structure for the information given in table 4.5. Use the column headings as the field names and set the appropriate data type.

Task 3
Enter the data shown in table 4.5.

Task 4
Save the database as **BLITZ**.

Task 5
There are two late entries in the competition, please add the following records to the database:

Team	Contact Name	Telephone	Paid
Yellow Wanderers	Daisy	4438903	Yes
Orange Peelers	Enda	6263486	No

Assignment 3

In Assignment 3 you will: •Enter field name •Select data type •Enter data •Save •**Search (1 condition).**

Table 4.6 shows information on students attending a Summer Camp.

Table 4.6

Surname	First Name	Telephone	DOB	Amount Paid	Swimmer
Jones	Gerry	08684569	16/12/93	€70.00	Yes
Walsh	Simon	08685569	25/03/94	€70.00	Yes
Smith	Keith	08569632	13/02/94	€65.00	No
Weir	Jenny	05698987	14/12/93	€60.00	Yes
Mann	Jack	06397892	27/11/93	€70.00	Yes
Durcan	Ann	04562365	25/12/93	€70.00	No

Task 1
Create a suitable database structure for the information given in table 4.6. Use the column headings as the field names and set the appropriate data type.
Task 2
Enter the data shown in table 4.6.
Task 3
Save the database as **CAMP**.
Task 4
Search the database for students who can swim. Save the query as **QRYSWIM**.
Task 5
The cost of the summer camp is €70.00. Search the database to find out which students have paid the full amount. Save the query as **QRYPAID**.

📄 **Note**

Using MS Access? If you are – save the table as TBLCAMP.

👉 **Tip**

If you save a query it can be run whenever you like, e.g. after you have added more records.

Assignment 4
In Assignment 4 you will: •Enter field name •Select data type •Enter data •**Save** •**Search (2 conditions)** •**Print.**

Table 4.7 shows information from Keane's Car Sales.

Task 1
Create a suitable database structure for the information given in table 4.7. Use the column headings as the field names and set the appropriate data type.
Task 2
Enter the data shown in table 4.7.
Task 3
Save the database as **CARSALES**.

Table 4.7

Model	Type	Colour	Miles
KA	1.3 3DR	Blue	21K
Escort	1.4LX 4DR	Green	35K
Focus	1.4LX 4DR	Silver	20K
Astra	1.4GL 4DR	Blue	40K
Astra	1.4GL 4DR	Blue	20K
Corsa	1.2 AUTO	Silver	19K
Mondeo	1.8LX 5DR	Black	22K
Mondeo	1.8LX 5DR	Blue	25K

👉 **Tip**

Press Ctrl '(i.e. hold down **Ctrl** while you press ') in a field to insert the same text or value as in the field above.

📄 **Note**

Using MS Access? If you are – save the table as TBLCARSALES.

Task 4
Search the database for blue cars. Save the query as **QRYBLUE**.
Task 5
Print out the result of the search.
Task 6
Search the database for blue cars with mileage less than 30K and print out the result. Save the query as **QRYCARSK**.

👉 **Tip**

Preview your page before printing to make sure that your printout will be what you expect.

Assignment 5

In Assignment 5 you will: •Enter field name •Select data type •Enter data •Save •**Search (2 conditions)** •Insert new data •**Delete record** •Print.

Table 4.8 shows information on some of the members of Dunkers Basketball Club.

Table 4.8

Surname	First Name	Age	Gender	Telephone
Evans	Dara	17	Female	2356987
Murphy	Mary	18	Female	2358976
Ellis	David	18	Male	2346935
Smith	Fern	16	Female	2346213
Doyle	Chloe	17	Female	2357891
Nolan	Jamie	17	Male	2345627
Walsh	Ed	19	Male	2358719
Byrne	Sam	16	Male	2345819

Task 1

Create a suitable database structure for the information given in table 4.8. Use the column headings as the field names and set the appropriate data type.

 Note

Using MS Access? If you are – save the table as TBLDUNKERS.

Task 2

Enter the data shown in table 4.8.

Task 3

Save the database as **DUNKERS**.

Task 4

Search the database for male members aged 17 and younger. Save the query as **QRY17U17**.

Task 5

Print out the result of the search.

Task 6

Add the following records to the database:

 Note

Records are deleted when they are no longer needed.

Surname	First Name	Age	Gender	Telephone
Evans	John	17	Male	2356987
Murphy	Gerry	16	Male	2358976
Ivers	Isobel	17	Female	2343535

Task 7

Mary Murphy has moved and is no longer a member of the club: remove her record from the database.

Task 8
Search the database for male and female members aged 17 and younger and print out the results of the search. Save the query as **QRYALL**.

Assignment 6
In Assignment 6 you will: •Enter field name •Select data type •Enter data •Save •Search •Sort data •Edit data.

Table 4.9 shows information from a Geography project on capital cities.

 Tip

Sorting involves putting the records in a file into a particular order e.g. alphabetical order

Table 4.9

Country	Capital	Air Distance from Dublin	Currency
Australia	Canberra	10842	Dollar
Canada	Ottawa	3600	Dollar
China	Beijing	5342	Yuan
New Zealand	Wellington	11971	Dollar
Russia	Moscow	1836	Rouble
South Africa	Pretoria	5881	Rand
United States	Washington DC	3944	Dollar
Spain	Madrid	1052	Euro
Germany	Berlin	860	Euro

Note

Using MS Access? If you are – save the table as TBLCAPITALS.

Task 1
Create a suitable database structure for the information given in table 4.9. Use the column headings as the field names and set the appropriate data type.
Task 2
Enter the data shown in table 4.9.
Task 3
Save the database as **CAPITALS**.
Task 4
Sort the data in alphabetical order by capital city.
Task 5
Search the database for countries that use the Euro as currency. Save the query as **QRYEURO**.
Task 6
Search the database for countries that are more than 10,000 air

miles away from Dublin and that use the Dollar as currency. Save the query as **QRYDOLLAR**.

Task 7

Berlin is 867 air miles from Dublin. Make this change in the database.

Assignment 7

In Assignment 7 you will: •**Open existing file** •Sort data •Save •Print.

Task 1

Open the database called **CAMP**. (Assignment 3)

Task 2

Sort the data by Date of Birth (DOB).

Task 3

Save the changes you have made.

Task 4

Print one copy of the database.

Assignment 8

In Assignment 8 you will: •Enter field name •Select data type •Enter data •Save •**Search (not)** •Sort data •Insert new records •Delete record •Print.

Table 4.10 shows information from Football Trips Ltd on their bookings for the month of November.

Table 4.10

Team	Destination	Cost	Stay/Nights
Man. United	Manchester	€359.00	1
Man. United	Barcelona	€599.00	2
Arsenal	London	€399.00	1
Arsenal	Amsterdam	€499.00	2
Chelsea	London	€389.00	1
Chelsea	London	€389.00	1
Leeds United	Leeds	€349.00	1
Liverpool	Rome	€599.00	2
Inter Milan	Milan	€559.00	2

Task 1
Create a suitable database structure for the information given in table 4.10. Use the column headings as the field names, set the appropriate data type and enter the data shown in the table.

Note

Using MS Access? If you are – save the table as TBLFOOTBALL.

Task 2
Save the database as **FOOTBALL**.

Task 3
Add the following records to the database:

Team	Destination	Cost	Stay/Nights
Man. United	London	€399.00	1
Liverpool	Liverpool	€399.00	1
Leeds United	Newcastle	€399.00	1

Task 4
Sort the data in alphabetical order by Team.

Task 5
Search the database for trips to London that cost less than €399.00.Save the query as **QRYLONDON**.

Task 6
Search the database for Arsenal matches that are not in London. Save the query as **QRYARSENAL**.

Task 7
The trip to see Inter Milan has been cancelled please remove this from the database.

Task 8
Sort the records according to cost.

Task 9
Print one copy of the database sorted by Destination.

Assignment 9

Table 4.11

In Assignment 9 you will:
•Enter field name •Select data type •Enter data •Save • **Search (wildcard)** •Sort data •**Add new field** •Insert new data.

Table 4.11 shows booking details for guests at Bertie's B&B.

Surname	Room No	Price Per Night
Dunne	10	€40.00
Kelly	1	€35.00
Murphy	3	€35.00
Scully	5	€35.00
Butler	11	€40.00
Byrne	16	€40.00
Kenny	8	€35.00

Task 1
Create a suitable database structure for the information

given in table 4.11. Use the column headings as the field names, set the appropriate data type and enter the data shown in the table.

Task 2

Save the database as **BERTIE**.

Task 3

Create a new field called Stay/Nights and enter the following information:

Stay/Nights
4
7
6
9
5
8
9

Task 4

Search for guests whose surname starts with the letter 'B'. Save the query as **QRYGUESTB**.

Task 5

Search for guests whose surname starts with the letter 'K'. Save the query as **QRYGUESTK**

Task 6

Sort the database by Stay/Nights and print one copy of the database.

Assignment 10

In Assignment 10 you will: •Open existing file •Add new field •Insert new data •**Search (3 conditions & Or)** •Sort Data •Save •Print.

Task 1

Open the database called **CARSALES**. (Assignment 4)

Task 2

Create a new field called **Make** before the **Model** field and enter the following information:

Ford, Ford, Ford, Opel, Opel, Opel, Ford, Ford.

Task 3

Search the database for blue Ford cars with less than 30K on the clock. Save the query as **QRYFORDU30K**.

Task 4

Sort the database by car colour.

Task 5

Search the database for Ford cars that are blue or green. Save the query as **QRYFORD**.

Task 6

Print one copy of the database.

Assignment 11

In Assignment 11 you will: •Enter field name •Select data type •Enter data •Save •Search (multiple conditions & not) •Add new field •Insert new data •Sort data •Print.

Table 4.12 shows information on forthcoming trips at Leadmore Mountaineering Club.

Table 4.12

Surname	First Name	Mweelrea	Twelve Pins	Errigal
Carthy	John	€17.00	€15.00	€25.00
Davis	Jack	€17.00		€25.00
Doyle	Aileen	€17.00	€15.00	
Neary	Paul	€17.00		€25.00
Neary	Kevin		€15.00	€25.00
Doyle	Josie	€17.00	€15.00	€25.00

Task 1
Create a suitable database structure for the information given in table 4.12. Use the column headings as the field names, set the appropriate data type and enter the data shown in the table.

Task 2
Save the database as **LMCLUB**.

Task 3
Create a new field called Donard. The cost of the trip to Donard is €27.00 and all the members are going. Enter this information in the database.

Task 4
Search the database for members who are going on all four trips. Save the query as **QRYTRIPX4**.

Task 5
Search the database for members who are going on the Errigal trip but not going on the Twelve Pins trip. Save the query as **QRYTRIPEG**.

Task 6
Sort the database in alphabetical order by members' surnames.

Task 7
Print one copy of the database.

Note

Using MS Access? If you are – save the table as TBLLMCLUB.

Assignment 12
In Assignment 12 you will: •Enter field name •Select data type •Enter data •Save •Add new field •Insert new data •Sort data •**Search (Between)** •Print **(landscape)**.

Action Aid Ballybay holds an annual charity mountain climb. Participants climb 3 mountains in 10 hours. Table 4.13 shows details of participants, climbing times and money raised.

Table 4.13

Climbers	Cruagh More	Comderagh	Cairn Beg	Amount Raised
Kemmy J	2:10	2:15	3:15	€1050.00
O'Hare M	2:12	2:34	3:05	€2345.00
Freely J J	2:05	2:20	3:12	€1230.00
Collins D	2:11	2:25	3:10	€6519.00
Kaffrey V	2:12	2:17	3:25	€1045.00
Neary P	2:07	2:20	3:16	€4562.00
Kenny M	2:04	2:27	3:22	€3756.00

Note

Using MS Access?
If you are – save
the table as
TBLBALLYBAY.

Tip

Don't type the
Euro symbol (€)
when entering a
query condition
in a **currency**
field.

Task 1

Create a suitable database structure for the information given in table 4.13. Use the column headings as the field names, set the appropriate data type and enter the data shown in the table.

Task 2

Save the database as **BALLYBAY**.

Task 3

Insert a new field called **Total Time** before the Amount Raised field and enter the following times:

7:40, 7:51, 7:37, 7:46, 7:54, 7:43, 7:53.

Task 4

Sort the database by fastest time.

Task 5

Search the database for participants who raised more than €1,045.00 and whose name starts with the letter 'K'. Save the query as **QRYAMOUNTK**.

Task 6

Search the database for climbers who had total climbing times between 7:36 and 7:50. Save the query as **QRYTIME** and print one copy with landscape orientation.

Assignment 13

In Assignment 13 you will: •Enter field name •Select data type •Enter data •Save •**Sort data by primary and secondary key fields** •Add new records •Search •Print.

Table 4.14 (on next page) shows a section of the bookings for Celtic Taxis.

Task 1

Create a suitable database structure for the information given in table 4.14. Use the column headings as the field names, set the appropriate data type and enter the data shown in the table.

Table 4.14

From	To	Distance	Time	Date	Fare
Esker	Leadmore	10	23:30	11/11	€20.00
Esker	Avondale	12	09:30	12/11	€24.00
Avondale	Deryvale	16	08:15	12/11	€32.00
Avondale	Mill Hill	5	07:45	12/11	€10.00
Deryvale	Mill Hill	9	10:00	12/11	€18.00
Mill Hill	Esker	25	07:15	13/11	€50.00
Mill Hill	Leadmore	27	06:30	13/11	€54.00

Note

Using MS Access?
If you are – save
the table as
TBLTAXI.

Task 2
Save the database as **TAXI**.
Task 3
Sort the database using the **DATE** field as the primary key and **TIME** as the secondary key field.
Task 4
There are some new bookings. Add the following records to the database:

From	To	Distance	Time	Date	Fare
Leadmore	Esker	10	09:30	14/11	€20.00
Esker	Mill Hill	25	17:50	11/11	€50.00
Mill Hill	Avondale	5	19:35	14/11	€10.00

Note

Some database
packages will not
allow you to sort
the database
using primary
and secondary
keys without first
doing a report –
if so, skip this
task for now.

Task 5
Resort the data in accordance with the instructions given in Task 3.
Task 6
Search the database for journeys from Mill Hill between 13/11 and 14/11. Save the query as **QRYDATE**.
Task 7
Search the database for journeys that took place on 11/11 or 14/11 between 9:00 a.m. and 9:00 p.m. Save the query as **QRYTIME**.
Task 8
Print out one copy of the database and one copy of each query.

Assignment 14
In Assignment 14 you will: •Enter field name •Select data type •Enter data •Save •Sort data by primary and secondary key fields •Delete field •Edit data •Search (multiple conditions) •Print.

Table 4.15 shows a section of the database that holds information on test results at Leadmore Community College.

Table 4.15

Surname	Name	Class	Halloween	Xmas	Easter	Summer
Byrne	Amy	1Red	72	63	70	67
Byrne	Joe	1Blue	75	67	85	58
Jones	Adam	2Red	87	80	80	78
Kelly	Tom	1Red	56	60	70	72
Court	Jack	2Red	65	59	65	70
Collins	Mick	1Blue	67	58	83	79
Barry	Tina	1Green	70	68	87	80
Jones	John	2Red	85	83	87	92

Note

Using MS Access? If you are – save the table as TBLRESULTS.

Tip

In a query with multiple conditions, add the first condition and then run the query to see if it works – then add the second condition and run the query again – continue like this until all conditions are added.

Task 1

Create a suitable database structure for the information given in table 4.15. Use the column headings as the field names, set the appropriate data type and enter the data shown in the table.

Task 2

Save the database as **RESULTS**.

Task 3

Sort the database using the **Surname** field as the primary key and **Class** as the secondary key field and print out one copy of the sorted information.

Task 4

The Halloween test results are no longer needed, delete this field from the database.

Task 5

The Xmas result for Joe Byrne, 1Blue should read 85, correct this mistake in the database.

Task 6

Search the database for pupils in 1Red, 1Blue and 1Green who scored less than 70 in the Xmas tests and more than 70 in the Easter tests. Save the query as **QRYMARKS**.

Task 7

Search the database for students who scored exactly 80 or 85 in each test. Save the queries as **QRYEXACTX** , **QRYEXACTE** and **QRYEXACTS** and print one copy of each query.

Assignment 15

In Assignment 15 you will: •Enter field name •Select data type **•Enter data using a data entry form** •Save •Sort data by primary and secondary key fields •Search.

Table 4.16 shows a section of a database that holds information on Patients at St Mary's Hospital, Leadmore.

Table 4.16

Name	Surname	Address	Telephone	Ward	Insurance	Admitted
John	Kerry	12 Church View	07863219	3G	Yes	05/06
Dara	Jones	23 High Street	07895632	1G	No	03/06
Ann	Kelly	34 Park Road	07894563	2G	No	06/06
Shane	Doherty	Ballybay	05673789	1G	Yes	04/06
Sarah	Kenny	17 Mountain Ct	07893652	1G	No	02/06
Teddy	Kennedy	Ballybay	05671234	3G	Yes	05/06
Mary	Murphy	9 St Johns Road	07892586	2G	Yes	03/06
Molly	Aitken	Ballybay	05672314	1G	No	05/06

Note

Forms allow you to type data into a database using a specially designed form rather than straight into a table.

Task 1
Use a data entry form to enter the records shown in table 4.16.
Task 2
Save the database as **STMARYS**.
Task 3
Sort the database using the **Ward** field as the primary key and **Insurance** as the secondary key field.
Task 4
Search the database for patients with an address in Ballybay and who have Insurance. Save the query as **QRYINS** and print one copy.
Task 5
Search the database for patients who do not have Ballybay in their address and were admitted between 03/06 and 05/06. Save the query as **QRYNOTBB** and print one copy.

Note

Using MS Access? If you are – save the table as TBLSTMARYS.

Assignment 16

In Assignment 16 you will: •Enter field name •Select data type •Enter data using a data entry form •Save **•Index** •Add new records • Search.

Table 4.17 shows a section of a database that holds information on Football world cup finals.

Table 4.17

Winner	Score	Runner Up	Result	Venue
Argentina	3	West Germany	2	Mexico City, Mexico
Brazil	5	Sweden	2	Stockholm, Sweden
Italy	3	West Germany	1	Madrid, Spain
Uruguay	4	Argentina	2	Montevideo, Uruguay
England	4	West Germany	2	London, England
Brazil	2	Germany	0	Yokohama, Japan
West Germany	3	Hungary	2	Bern, Switzerland
Uruguay	2	Brazil	1	Rio de Janeiro, Brazil

Task 1
Use a data entry form to enter the records shown in table 4.17.
Task 2
Save the database as **WORLDCUP**.
Task 3
Insert a new field called **Year** before the Winner field and enter the following information 1986, 1958, 1982, 1930, 1966, 2002, 1954 and 1950.
Task 4
Create an index using the **Year** field.
Task 5
Add the following records to the database:

Year	Winner	Score	Runner Up	Score	Venue
1938	Italy	4	Hungary	2	Paris, France
1970	Brazil	4	Italy	1	Mexico City, Mexico
1998	France	3	Brazil	0	Paris, France

Task 6
Search the database for winners since 1958, excluding Brazil. Save the query as **QRYWINXB** and print one copy.
Task 7 (Optional)
The first world cup final was played in 1930 and the tournament has taken place every four years since then with the exception of 1942 and 1946. Some records are missing from the database. Use the Internet to find the missing information and insert it in the database.

Assignment 17

In Assignment 17 you will: •Enter field name •Select data type •Enter data using a data entry form •Save •Index •Add new records •Search •Print.

Table 4.18 shows a section of a stock database for washing lines at Healy's Home Store.

Table 4.18

Code	Length of Line	Spear	Cover	Rotating Diameter	Guarantee	Price
4504670	38 m	Yes	No	185 cm	2 years	€32.99
4504704	60 m	Yes	Yes	307 cm	10 years	€45.99
4504687	40 m	Yes	Yes	250 cm	5 years	€26.99
4504292	38 m	Yes	Yes	254 cm	4 years	€54.99
4504168	45 m	Yes	No	264 cm	3 years	€49.99

Task 1
Use a data entry form to enter the records shown in table 4.18.
Task 2
Save the database as **LINES**.
Task 3
Create an index using the **Code** field.
Task 4
Add the following records to the database:

Code	Length of Line	Spear	Cover	Rotating Diameter	Guarantee	Price
4504302	58 m	Yes	No	289 cm	5 years	€69.99
4505040	45 m	Yes	No	317 cm	10 years	€75.99
4504312	48 m	Yes	Yes	256 cm	5 years	€42.99

Task 5
Search the database for lines with a cover costing less than €50.00. Save the query as **QRYLINES** and print one copy in landscape orientation.
Task 6
Search the database for lines that are less than 50 m in length and have a 5-year guarantee. Save the query as **QRYGUART** and print one copy in landscape orientation.

Note

Using MS Access? If you are – save the table as TBLLINES.

Tip

Don't type the Euro symbol (€) when entering a query condition in a **currency** field.

Task 7
The Diameter field is no longer required delete this field from the database.
Task 8
Print out the complete database in landscape orientation.

Assignment 18
In Assignment 18 you will: •Enter field name •Select data type •Enter data using a data entry form •Save •Index •Add new records •Search •**Find and replace** •Print.
Table 4.19 shows details of swimming lessons at Leadmore Swimming Pool.

Table 4.19

Day	Time	Level	Instructor	Cost	Duration
Tuesday	4:00–4:30	Beginner	Quinn	€55.00	10 weeks
Tuesday	4:30–5:00	Intermediate	Quinn	€65.00	10 weeks
Tuesday	8:00–8:30	Advanced	Dunne	€70.00	10 weeks
Monday	4:00–4:30	Beginner	Dunne	€55.00	8 weeks
Monday	4:30–5:00	Beginner	Dunne	€55.00	8 weeks
Monday	8:00–8:30	Intermediate	Quinn	€55.00	8 weeks
Saturday	1:00–1:30	Advanced	Dunne	€70.00	10 weeks

Task 1
Use a data entry form to enter the records shown in table 4.19.
Task 2
Save the database as **SWIM**.

Note

Using MS Access?
If you are – save
the table as
TBLSWIM.

Task 3
Create an index using the **Level** field.
Task 4
Due to high demand more classes have been organised. Add the following records to the database.

Day	Time	Level	Instructor	Cost	Duration
Wednesday	4:00–4:30	Beginner	Quinn	€55.00	10 weeks
Wednesday	4:30–5:00	Intermediate	Quinn	€65.00	10 weeks
Tuesday	8:30–9:00	Advanced	Dunne	€70.00	10 weeks
Monday	7:30–8:00	Beginner	Dunne	€55.00	8 weeks

Task 5
Due to maintenance work the pool will not be available on

Tuesday so these classes have been changed to Thursday. Use the find and replace facility to make the necessary changes to the database.

Task 6

Sort the database by the **Day** field and then by the **Time** field.

Task 7

Search the database for beginner and intermediate classes on Mondays or Wednesdays. Save the query as **QRYCLASS** and print out the results.

Note

Find and **Replace** allows you to tell the database to look for one word and replace it with another.

Assignment 19

In Assignment 19 you will: •Enter field name •Select data type •Enter data using a data entry form •Save •Find and replace •**Produce report (all fields)** •Print.

Table 4.20 shows details of classes at Ballybay Leisure Centre.

Table 4.20

Day	Activity	Start	Finish	Level	Instructor	Cost
Monday	Yoga	10:00	10:45	Beginners	Keane	€5.00
Tuesday	Circuit	19:00	19:45	None	Murphy	€3.50
Monday	Spinning	11:00	11:45	Beginners	Daly	€5.00
Wednesday	Spinning	19:00	19:45	Intermediate	Daly	€5.00
Friday	Yoga	10:00	10:45	Beginners	Keane	€5.00
Thursday	Circuit	20:00	20:45	None	Murphy	€3.50
Friday	Spinning	19:00	19:45	Advanced	Daly	€5.00
Thursday	Aerobics	10:00	10:45	Low Impact	Murphy	€4.00
Wednesday	Aerobics	10:00	10:45	High Impact	Daly	€4.00

Task 1

Use a data entry form to enter the records shown in table 4.20.

Task 2

Save the database as **KEEPFIT**.

Task 3

The instructor Daly has left and has been replaced by a new instructor called Moloney. Use the find and replace facility to make the necessary changes to the database.

Task 4

Classes that are due to start at 10:00 a.m. have been changed to start at 10:15 a.m. This means their finish time also changes by 15 minutes. Use the find and replace facility to make the necessary changes to the database.

Note

Using MS Access? If you are – save the table as TBLKEEPFIT.

Note

Reports allow
you to present
data in a wide
variety of ways.
They can be
based on the
database or on a
query.

Task 5
Sort the database by the **Day** field then by the **Start** field and then by the **Finish** field.

Task 6
The Leisure Centre manager has asked you to produce a report displaying all the information in the database. The report title is 'Keep Fit Classes'.

Task 7
Print one copy of the report.

Assignment 20

In Assignment 20 you will: •Enter field name •Select data type •Enter data using a data entry form •Save •Search •Change field name •Produce report (selected fields) •Print.

Table 4.21 shows details of stock on order for Little Angels Nursery store.

Table 4.21

Item	Code	Quantity	Price	Order Date	Delivered
Cot	CO805	5	€250.00	03/01	Yes
Cot	CO810	3	€299.00	03/01	No
Cot-bed	CB820	2	€350.00	15/01	No
Pram	PR209	10	€220.00	10/01	No
Rock a tot	RT505	15	€85.00	03/01	Yes
Pram	PR210	20	€250.00	03/01	Yes
Play Gym	PG220	9	€35.00	03/01	No
Car Seat	CS203	12	€180.00	03/01	No
Rock a tot deluxe	RT510	14	€125.00	09/01	Yes
Mobile	MO930	6	€30.00	09/01	No
Car seat deluxe	CS210	13	€210.00	03/01	Yes
Mobile	MO860	8	€35.00	03/01	Yes

 Note

Using MS Access?
If you are – save
the table as
TBLANGELS.

Task 1
Use a data entry form to enter the records shown in table 4.21 and create an index using the Code field.

Task 2
Save the database as **ANGELS**.

Task 3
Search the database for products ordered between 03/01 and 09/01 that have been delivered. Save the query as **QRYDEL** and print one copy.

Task 4
Change the name of the Item field to Product.
Task 5
The manager has just discovered that product code MO930 has been delivered, change this on the database.
Task 6
Produce a report linked to the query displaying Code, Delivered and Price information only. The report title is 'Little Angels Deliveries'.

Assignment 21
In Assignment 21 you will: •Enter field name •Select data type •Enter data using a data entry form •Save •Search •Produce report •Print.

Table 4.22 shows some of the information gathered as part of a school project on satellites.

Table 4.22

Launched	Nation	Name	Type	Satellite Accomplishments
04/10/1957	USSR	Sputnik 1	Scientific	1st to orbit earth
01/04/1960	US	Tiros 1	Weather	1st weather satellite photographic system
10/07/1962	US	Telstar	Communication	1st to relay TV programmes between US and Europe
31/01/1958	US	Explorer 1	Scientific	1st American satellite
06/04/1965	US	Early Bird	Communication	1st commercial communication satellite
03/11/1957	USSR	Sputnik 2	Scientific	1st to carry an animal
18/12/1958	US	Project Score	Communication	Broadcast 1st voice messages from space
17/02/1959	US	Vanguard 2	Weather	1st to send weather information back to Earth
23/04/1965	USSR	Molniya	Communication	1st USSR communication satellite

Task 1
Use a data entry form to enter the records shown in table 4.22 and create an index using the Type field.
Task 2
Save the database as **SATELLITE**.

Note

Using MS Access?
If you are – save
the table as
TBLSATELLITES.

Task 3

Search the database for US satellites launched before 1961. Save the query as **QRYUS** and print one copy in landscape orientation.

Task 4

Produce a report linked to this query displaying Nation, Launched, Name and Type information only. The report title is 'US Satellites before 1961'.

Task 5

Search the database for satellites other than those launched by the US. Save the query as **QRYNOTUS** and produce a report linked to this query displaying Nation, Name and Satellite Accomplishments only. The report title is 'Satellites not launched by US'.

 Note

Using MS Access? If you are – open the table TBLBALLYBAY.

Assignment 22

In Assignment 22 you will: •Open existing file •Produce report (showing Total figure) •Print.

Task 1

Open the database called **Ballybay**. (Assignment 12)

Task 2

You have been asked to produce a report showing all the information in the database. The report title is 'Action Aid Ballybay'.

Task 3

Insert a total for the Amount Raised field in the report.

Task 4

Print one copy of the report.

 Note

Using MS Access? If you are – open the table TBLTAXI.

Assignment 23

In Assignment 23 you will: •Open existing file •Produce report (showing Total figure) •Print.

Task 1

Open the database called **Taxi**. (Assignment 13)

Task 2

You have been asked to produce a report showing all the information in the database. The report title is 'Celtic Taxis'.

Task 3

Insert a total for the **Fare** field in the report.

Task 4

Print one copy of the report.

Assignment 24

In Assignment 24 you will: •Open existing file •Produce report (showing average figure) •Print.

Task 1
Open the database called **RESULTS**. (Assignment 14)

Task 2
You have been asked to produce a report showing all the information in the database. The report title is 'Leadmore CC Results'.

Task 3
Insert an average results figure for the Xmas, Easter and Summer fields in the report.

Task 4
Print one copy of the report.

 Note

Using MS Access?
If you are – open
the table
TBLRESULTS.

Assignment 25

In Assignment 25 you will: •Enter field name •Select data type •Enter data using a data entry form •Save •Search •Produce and print labels.

Table 4.23 shows a section of the voting register in Ballybay.

Table 4.23

Title	First Name	Surname	Address 1	Address 2
Mrs	Ann	Daly	2 Church View	Ballybay
Mr	Richard	Kelly	87 High Street	Ballybay
Ms	Jenny	Jones	76 Martins Lane	Ballybay
Dr	Nora	Ruane	The Old Mill	Ballybay
Mr	Michael	Murphy	4 Church View	Ballybay

Task 1
Use a data entry form to enter the records shown in table 4.23.

Task 2
Save the database as **REGISTER**.

Task 3
Create an index using the Surname field.

Task 4
Add the following records to the database:

Title	First Name	Surname	Address 1	Address 2
Mr	Tom	Byrne	2 High Street	Ballybay
Mrs	Mary	Kelly	87 High Street	Ballybay

 Note

Using MS Access?
If you are – save
the table as
TBLREGISTER.

Task 5

One of the election candidates has asked you to produce labels for everyone in the database so that she can send a letter to each voter. Create the labels to fit two-across an A4 page.

Task 6

Print the labels.

Assignment 26

In Assignment 26 you will: •Enter field name •Select data type •Enter data using a data entry form •Save •Search •Produce and print labels.

Table 4.24 shows details of people registered for Saturday swimming lessons at Leadmore Swimming Pool.

Table 4.24

Surname	First Name	Address 1	Address 2	Paid
Ellis	Eileen	3 High Street	Leadmore	Yes
Collins	Tom	12 Baroda Court	Leadmore	No
Tracey	Enda	15 Greenhills	Leadmore	Yes
Purcell	Amy	6 Mountain View	Leadmore	No
Lynch	Jack	3 Connell Drive	Leadmore	No
Durcan	Denise	5 The Mall	Leadmore	No

Task 1

Use a data entry form to enter the records shown in table 4.24.

Task 2

Save the database as **SATURDAY**.

Task 3

Create an index using the Surname field.

Task 4

Search the database for those who have not paid. Save the query as **QRYNOPAY** and print one copy in landscape orientation.

Task 5

Create a mailing label for each person who has not paid using the First Name, Surname, Address 1 and Address 2 fields only.

Task 6

Print the labels.

Unit 5 – Internet and E-mail

1. The Internet

The Internet is made up of a large number of computers all over the world connected together by telephone lines. It allows computer users to share and exchange information with each other. You can do many things on the Internet e.g. look up information, go shopping, download pictures, text, music and software; send and receive e-mail messages as well as watch live television pictures.

Connecting to the Internet

The most common way of connecting to the Internet is through a computer that has a modem and web-browsing software and is connected to a telephone line. An ordinary telephone line is fine but you can choose to connect via an **ISDN** line or by **Broadband**, both of which are considerably faster than an ordinary telephone line. You can also connect through some mobile phones; in addition some TV services offer access to the Internet and e-mail through the television without the need for a computer at all.

Once you have chosen a method of communication, you then have to find an **Internet Service Provider (ISP)**. This is a company which provides you with access to the Internet such as Eircom, Ireland On-Line (IOL) or Indigo. Internet service providers differ widely, so it can pay to shop around and make sure you get the best deal.

2. The World Wide Web (WWW)

This is the best-known part of the Internet, often just called the Web. It is made up of millions of web pages stored on computers all over the world. Individuals and organisations provide their own pages of information, which begin as their **home page**; this is the page that appears first when someone accesses your website.

A special type of link, called a **hyperlink**, allows you to move from one web page to another. There are two types of hyperlinks **internal** and **external**. An internal hyperlink brings you to another page in the same website and an external hyperlink brings you to a web page (normally the home page) of a different website. When you move the mouse pointer around the screen, the shape changes from an arrow to a hand when it is over a hyperlink.

Browsers

The easiest way to look at or surf the Internet is to look at web pages with a program called a browser. The most commonly used browsers are Microsoft Internet Explorer and Netscape Navigator.

Searching the Web

A **search engine** is a program that helps you to find information on the Web. Search engines compile their listings by using either people or special programs known as **crawlers** and can be divided into the following three different types:

(i) Directories: These are compiled by people and so contain only information that is relevant to each category. A directory looks for information by subject matter, so that you can browse as in a library. Examples of directories are **Yahoo**, **Onekey** and **Looksmart**.

(ii) Automated Search Engines: These are compiled by special software known as **crawlers, spiders** or **bots** which continually run all over the Web collecting **keywords** from each website. They are good for finding very specific information but very often show up unwanted information also! Examples of this type of search engine are **AltaVista**, **Google** and **Excite**.

(iii) Meta Search Engines: These work by sending your query to a number of search engines at the same time and then list the results in one location. Examples of this type of search engine are **Ask Jeeves** and **Go2Net**.

Internet Addresses

Every web page has a unique address known as a **URL** (Uniform Resource Locator). Most URLs start with **http://www.** followed by a specific site address which can be subdivided with full stops and forward slashes(/). A typical address is:

http://www.rte.ie

http:// is the protocol used and stands for Hypertext Transfer Protocol. This is the set of rules used by the Internet for sending and receiving data between computers. Usually, it is not necessary to type in http:// as the browser adds it automatically.

www means World Wide Web and is found in most, but not all, web pages.

'**rte.ie**' is the **domain name** showing the organisation that has the site (in this case RTE) and '.ie' reveals the country of origin, Ireland.

Website addresses often indicate whether the site is commercial with either '**.co**' or '**.com**', a government organisation with '**.gov**', or an academic organisation with '**.ac**'.

Figure 5.1: The address box

3. E-mail

E-mail (or electronic mail) is used to send messages from one computer to another. You type a message into your computer, enter the recipient's e-mail address, click the 'Send' button and it is transferred over the Internet, arriving almost instantaneously anywhere in the world.

Server-based E-mail

When you sign up with an Internet Service Provider (ISP), you are usually given an e-mail address free of charge. One of the most widely used programs to access such accounts is called Outlook Express. With this program you can connect to the Internet to send any messages you have written while any new ones will be transferred to your computer. Once that is done you can disconnect from the Internet. The advantage of this is that you can read and write messages without being 'on-line'.

Web-based E-mail

With some types of Internet account, you access your e-mail from a website and your messages are kept on the web server, this is known as web-based e-mail. This means you have to be on-line for longer while you deal with them but the advantage is that you can check your mail from any computer anywhere on the Internet. This can be really useful when travelling. One of the most popular web-based e-mail services is Microsoft Hotmail. One advantage that Hotmail has over other web-based e-mail services is that it can be accessed through Outlook Express.

E-mail Addresses

E-mail addresses are similar to website addresses and are made up in much the same way. The format is always:

username@domain.name

Here the **username** is you and **domain.name** is the Internet Service Provider (ISP), or a website address.

Tom Walsh's personal address might look like this:

tom-walsh@eircom.net
or
tomwalsh@hotmail.com

An e-mail address cannot contain spaces and is usually in lower case. The address must be entered correctly or the message will come back to you marked 'undelivered'.

Components of an E-mail Program

All e-mail programs have the following similar components:

- New Mail/Compose – this is where you write your message.
- Reply – here you can reply to a message you have received.
- Forward – you can forward a copy of a message you have received to another person.
- Organise – you can file messages in different folders to help you stay organised.
- Delete – here you can delete messages you don't want to keep.
- Print – you can send the message to print.
- Attachments – here you can attach files created in other programs to an e-mail e.g. a spreadsheet.

Figure 5.2: Writing an e-mail message

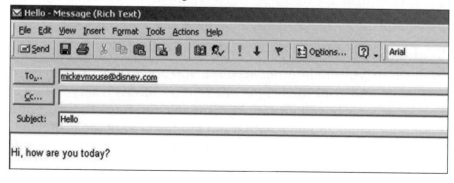

Internet and E-mail Security

Going 'on-line' is not without its dangers, therefore it is important to ensure that your PC or network has protection against electronic attacks.

These come in different forms, with the most common being the computer **virus**. While using an infected disk can pose a threat to your system the commonest way that viruses are transmitted is through e-mail, in particular e-mail attachments. Open the attachment and your computer will be infected. This has a knock-on effect in that many viruses will then forward themselves to friends and colleagues listed in your address book pretending to be genuine messages.

Viruses can be dealt with by using **anti-virus** software. Most virus-checking programs come complete with an 'on-line virus check' which checks e-mails and files for viruses as they are downloaded and alerts the user if any are detected. However the problem with some e-mail viruses is that they spread so rapidly that most of the damage has already been done before virus-checking software has been updated to deal with them.

Internet users can also be at risk from **hackers**. Hackers can gain access to any computer that is at the other end of an open connection to the Internet. Protecting your computer against this kind of threat requires the installation of a personal **firewall**. A firewall's job is to look at all incoming and outgoing Internet communications and to block anything that is unauthorised.

Physical Security

Physical security means protecting data by restricting access to the computers on which the data is being stored. In schools this is usually done by password protecting computers and locking computer room doors.

Spam

Spam is the sending of unsolicited e-mails. Sometimes these can be innocent enough, however, in a lot of cases they are sent in their hundreds just to annoy. The spammers obtain address lists by dubious means and generate more at random by putting a list of given names onto a domain name. To sidestep this you can replace letters with numbers in your address.

4. Shopping On-line

You can use the Internet for buying various things and it is also a great consumer guide. You can pay by credit or debit card and as long as you enter the payment details on a secure site it seems to be reasonably safe. If you are worried about on-line fraud but would still like to shop on-line you could have a credit card with a small credit limit for on-line purchases.

5. Internet and E-mail Assignments 1-19

Note: In the following assignments various website addresses (URLs) are given. Nothing stays the same for long on the Internet and you may find that when you come to use these assignments some addresses may no longer exist, they may have changed or some page layouts may be different. If this should be the case a simple search will find alternative addresses for you and you may learn something new along the way.

Assignment 1

In assignment 1 you will: **•Connect to Internet •Enter domain name •Add to Favorites •Select links •Return to home page**.

Note

Directories are compiled by people and organised by subject matter – examples include Yahoo, Onekey and Looksmart.

Task 1
Open your **Browser** and connect to the Internet.
Task 2
Type **www.search.irl.com** in the address box and click **Go**.
Task 3
Bookmark the address by adding it to your **Favorites** list.
Task 4
Select a main directory on **Counties** and then select a county of your choice. Have a look at some of the references by clicking on the links.
Task 5
Return to your home page.

Assignment 2

In assignment 2 you will: **•**Connect to Internet **•**Enter domain name **•**Enter keywords **•Print findings •**Return to home page.

Task 1
Type **www.yellowpages.ie** in the address box and click **Go**.
Task 2
Enter the name of the product/service you are searching for. For

the purpose of this exercise let's search for **Chinese Restaurants**.

Task 3

Enter the location of the restaurant e.g. **Castlebar** and click **Search**.

Task 4

Print one copy of your findings.

Task 5

Return to your home page.

Assignment 3

In assignment 3 you will: •Connect to Internet •Enter domain name •Enter keywords •Print findings •Return to home page.

You have decided to go on a short rail break to visit relatives.

Task 1

Type **www.irishrail.ie** in the address box and click **Go**.

Task 2

Enter the name of the station you will be travelling from.

Task 3

Enter a destination of your choice.

Task 4

Select the date and preferred time of travel and click **Go**.

Task 5

Click on **Details** to get more information on the journey time, number of changes and validity.

Task 6

Print a copy of your findings.

Assignment 4

In assignment 4 you will: •Connect to Internet •Enter domain name •Add to Favorites •**Add to Links toolbar** •Enter keywords •Select links •Print findings •Return to home page.

If you want information on a subject and your home dictionaries and encyclopaedias are not up to the job, Bartleby (www.bartleby.com) and Encarta (http://Encarta.msn.co.uk) are both free.

Task 1

Type **www.bartleby.com** in the address box and click **Go**.

Task 2

Bookmark the address by adding it to your **Favorites** list and put the site on your **Links** toolbar. You may need to shorten the name for this.

Tip

Closing your browser does not automatically disconnect you from the Internet – you have to instruct the computer to disconnect.

Tip

Another good travel site is **www. buseireann.ie**.

Tip

The Links toolbar, found under the address bar is a handy and visible place to store some of the sites you use most.

Task 3

In the search box type in the words **Civil War** and click **Go**.

Task 4

Have a look at some of the references by clicking on the links.

Task 5

Print one page of your findings.

Task 6

Return to your home page.

Assignment 5

In assignment 5 you will: •Connect to Internet •Enter domain name •Enter keywords •**Refine search** •Select links •**Save to folder** •Return to home page.

Note

Automated search engines are good for finding very specific information but very often show up unwanted information also! – examples include AltaVista, Google and Excite.

Task 1

Type **www.altavista.co.uk** in the address box and click **Go**.

Task 2

Suppose you wanted to find out about holiday mobile home rental in Scotland. In the search box enter the keywords **mobile home** and click **Find**.

Task 3

AltaVista finds hundreds of listings including in this case many mobile phone websites, with some in other languages. You therefore need to refine your search. Change the keyword in the search box to 'mobile homes' in quotes, set the language to **English** and click **Find**.

Task 4

There are still a lot of sites that are not directly relevant since we are not interested in France and Spain. You can tell AltaVista to exclude these by adding a keyword with a minus in front. Similarly if you are particularly interested in a topic such as 'rental' and 'Scotland' you can add keywords with a plus in front. In the search box add +rental+Scotland.

Task 5

Have a look at some of the references by clicking on the links.

Task 6

Save your results to a folder on your computer or a disk.

Task 7

Close the search engine and return to your home page.

Tip

Sometimes a website switches to another address.

Assignment 6

In assignment 6 you will: •Connect to Internet •Enter domain name •Enter keywords •Refine search •Select links •Print findings •Add to Links toolbar •Return to home page.

Task 1

Enter **www.google.ie** in the address box and click **Google Search**.

Task 2

Add it to Favorites.

Task 3

Type **Dail Eireann** into the search box and click the **Google Search** button. Google comes back with some links to **www.irlgov.ie** of which the home page is at the top.

Task 4

Click the first link to look at the Dail Eireann site.

Google results are consistently so relevant that they provide an alternative button **I'm Feeling Lucky** that takes you straight to the first result without seeing the list.

Task 5

Go back to the Google home page.

Task 6

This time you are going to look for a cooking recipe for fudge. In the search box, enter **fudge** and click **Google Search**.

This finds a huge number of references but mostly for games and music and some are not in English.

Task 7

Refine the search by including **recipes**. You can do this by using '+' as before or you could use the Advanced Search link.

Task 8

Click the Advanced Search link, fill in the boxes and click **Google Search**.

Task 9

Have a look at some of the references by clicking on the links and print out a recipe from one of the links.

Task 10

Add **Google** to your **Links** bar and return to your home page.

Assignment 7

In assignment 7 you will: •**Work off-line** •**Organise Favorites**.

Task 1

Open your **Browser** and select the button **Work Offline**.

Tip

Using MS Internet Explorer? If you are – to go to an address in the format www.name.com, just type the name, hold down Ctrl and press Enter. The rest is put in for you!

Tip

The **Language** box lets you specify pages in English only.

Task 2

In your **Browser**, click **Favorites** on the toolbar.

Task 3

Click on **Organise Favorites**.

The entries in the **Favorites** list appear in the order that they were added and you are going to reorganise them.

Task 4

Select **Bartleby** on the list.

Task 5

Create a folder called **Reference** and move Bartleby into this folder.

Task 6

Click the **Close** button.

Assignment 8

In assignment 8 you will: •Work off-line •**View History**.

Task 1

Open your **Browser** and select the button **Work Offline**.

Task 2

In your **Browser**, click **History** on the toolbar.

Task 3

Click the arrow next to **View** and select **By Date**.

Task 4

Widen the **History** window pane if you need to.

Task 5

Select the **Today** icon.

Task 6

A recent site you visited was **www.google.ie**, click on the name. The list now shows all the pages visited on that site.

Task 7

Open some of the other days and see where you or someone else has been browsing lately.

Task 8

Close the **History** list and return to your home page.

Assignment 9

In assignment 9 you will: •Connect to Internet •Enter domain name •Enter keywords •Select links •**Copy and paste findings** •Print •Return to home page.

Task 1

Open your **Browser** and connect to the Internet.

Task 2
Enter **www.howstuffworks.com** in the address box and click **Go**.

Task 3
In the search box, enter **laser printers** and click **Go**.

Task 4
Have a look at some of the references by clicking on the links.

Task 5
Copy your findings to a word document. You may need to copy the graphics separately.

Task 6
Save the word document as **LASER** and print one copy.

Task 7
Return to your home page.

Assignment 10
In assignment 10 you will: •Connect to Internet •Open Favorites •Enter keywords •Select links •**Download image** •Save •Return to home page.

It is possible to download pictures, video clips, sounds and software from the Internet. In assignments 10 and 11 you will download and save pictures and sounds. You will have to remember where you saved them so you may need to create some new folders or use a disk.

Task 1
Open your **Browser** and connect to the Internet.

Task 2
Open the **Favorites** list and choose **AltaVista**.

Task 3
Select **Images**. Suppose you were looking for pictures of Woodpeckers you would enter the word 'Woodpecker' in the **Find This** box.

Task 4
AltaVista returns a large number of images. Most of them are copyright but some are free. Select a suitable free image to download.

Task 5
Save the picture to a folder or disk.

Task 6
Download another free image and save it.

Task 7
Return to the **AltaVista** home page.

 Tip

If you want to know how your DVD player, fridge or computer works, it's all here.

📄 **Note**

You can only copy from this or any other site for your own personal use.

📄 **Note**

There is always a risk that a file you download from the Internet may be infected with a **virus** – if in doubt, **don't** download!

📄 **Note**

Many images are not free to copy – a popup message may warn you of this when you run the mouse pointer over them – otherwise clicking on an image will give further details.

Assignment 11

In assignment 11 you will: •Connect to Internet •Open Favorites •Enter keywords •Select links •**Download sound** •Save •Return to home page.

Tip

Check your speakers or headphones are switched on and the volume is turned up.

Task 1

Make sure you are still in the **www.altavista.ie** site.

Task 2

Select **MP3/Audio,** enter the word 'Woodpecker' in the **Find This** box and click **Search.**

Task 3

Have a look at some of the results.

Task 4

Sounds can be played on most modern computers, click on the Media icon if you have one and then select the sound file you want to hear.

Tip

Some links simply play a sound file without downloading it, this is known as **streaming** – many sites offer streamed music.

Task 5

Save the sound file to a folder or disk.

Task 6

Download another free sound file and save it.

Task 7

Return to the **AltaVista** home page.

Assignment 12

In assignment 12 you will: •Connect to Internet •Enter domain name •**Create e-mail account** •**Compose e-mail** •**Send e-mail** •**Save address** •Return to home page.

In assignments 12, 13, 14 and 15 you will send and receive e-mail. In order to do these assignments **your teacher will have to create a web-based e-mail account to which you can send your e-mail messages.**

Task 1

Open your **Browser** and connect to the Internet.

Task 2

There are numerous free web-based e-mail services. Your teacher will tell you the address of the one they want you to use.

Task 3

Use this service to create your own web-based e-mail account.

Task 4

Send the following e-mail message to the e-mail address that your teacher has provided.

> **Subject:** Trip to Leadmore Adventure Centre
>
> Hi
> Just a reminder to say the trip to Leadmore will take place in two weeks' time; you already have all the details. The train leaves at 8:30 a.m. so we are all going to meet at 8:15 at the station. Be there on time!
>
> Regards
> Rebecca

 Note

There is always a risk that an e-mail attachment may be infected with a **virus** – if in doubt, **don't** open it!

Task 5
Save the e-mail address you are sending the message to in your e-mail address book.

Task 6
Return to your home page.

Note

The Address Book is used to save the addresses of people you regularly send messages to – so that you don't have to type in their address each time.

Assignment 13
In assignment 13 you will: •Create and save word processing document •Access e-mail •Compose e-mail •**Attach file** •Send e-mail •Return to home page.

Task 1
Enter the following text in a new word processing document.

> ### Leadmore Itinerary
>
> **Day 1**
> - Train to Leadmore
> - Bus to Centre
> - Lunch
> - Canoeing/abseiling/hillwalking
> - Treasure Hunt
> - Dinner
> - Entertainment
>
> **Day 2**
> - Breakfast
> - Surfing/hillwalking/indoor pursuits
> - Lunch
> - Outdoor or indoor pursuits
> - Dinner
> - Entertainment
>
> **Day 3**
> - Breakfast

- ■ Outdoor pursuits
- ■ Bus to station
- ■ Train home

Task 2
Save the file as **Itinerary**.
Task 3
Log on to your web-based e-mail account and compose the following e-mail message.

> Subject: Trip to Leadmore Adventure Centre
>
> Hi There
> Please find attached the Itinerary for the Leadmore trip as requested.
>
> Regards
>
> Rebecca

Task 4
Attach the **Itinerary** file that you created on your word processor to the e-mail message.
Task 5
Send the e-mail message and attachment to the e-mail address provided by your teacher. Check your e-mail address book; you should have saved the e-mail address in assignment 12.

Assignment 14

In assignment 14 you will: •Access e-mail •**Check for new mail** •**Create new folder** •**Move mail between folders** •Return to home page.

For this assignment your teacher or another student will have sent the following message to your e-mail account.

> Subject: Paper Wastage
>
> Dear Student,
> To help reduce the running costs of the computer room and save a few trees at the same time, I would be grateful if you

would use both the print preview option and the spell checker before you print a document.

Many thanks for your co-operation

Lorraine Carolan
ICT Teacher

Task 1
Log on to your web-based e-mail account.

Task 2
Check for any new mail. The message above should be in your Inbox folder.

Task 3
In your e-mail program create a new mailbox or folder called **Teacher**.

Task 4
Move the message you received from your Inbox to this new folder.

Note

Make sure you have an up-to-date virus checker installed. It is a good idea not to open files with **.exe**, **.scr** or **.vbs** extensions unless you are expecting them.

Assignment 15
In assignment 15 you will: •Access e-mail •Compose e-mail •Attach file •Send e-mail •Save address •Return to home page.

Task 1
Log on to your web-based e-mail account and compose the following message:

Subject: Woodpecker sound

Hi There
Guess what? I was able to locate that woodpecker sound that was proving so elusive, please check out the attached file.

Regards

Jenny

Task 2
Attach the sound file that you saved as part of assignment 11 to the e-mail message.

Task 3

Send the e-mail message and attachment to the e-mail address of
one of your classmates.

Task 4

Save their e-mail address in your e-mail address book.

Assignment 16

In assignment 16 you will: •Connect to Internet •Enter domain
name •**Search for products** •**Select product** •Print •Return to home
page.

In assignments 16, 17, 18 and 19 you will learn how to use the
Internet to window shop.

Task 1

Open your **Browser** and connect to the Internet.

Task 2

Go to the site **www.buy4now.ie**.

Task 3

From the list of stores select a shop and search for a product of
your choice.

Task 4

Select the product and print out its details.

Task 5

Return to your home page.

Assignment 17

In assignment 17 you will: •Connect to Internet •Enter domain
name •Search for products •Select products •**Copy information to
WP document** •Send e-mail.

You want to buy some CDs from an on-line music store e.g.
www.cd-wow.com or **www.amazon.com**.

Task 1

Find two different CDs by an artist or band of your choice.

Task 2

Print out the details of each CD with their respective prices.

Task 3

Find the overall price of the two CDs including postage and
packaging.

Task 4

Copy the information to a word processing document and save
the document as **CD**.

Task 5
Send an e-mail message to a classmate and attach the file **CD** to it.

Assignment 18
In assignment 18 you will: •Connect to Internet •Enter domain name •Search for products •Select products •Copy information to WP document •Send e-mail.

You want to buy a book on **web design** from an on-line bookstore e.g. **www.gillmacmillan.ie** or **www.amazon.com**.

Task 1
Find two different books on web design.
Task 2
Print out the details of each book with their respective prices.
Task 3
Find the overall price of the two books including postage and packaging.
Task 4
Copy the information to a word processing document and save the document as **WEBDES**.
Task 5
Send an e-mail message to a classmate and attach the file **WEBDES** to it.

Assignment 19
In assignment 19 you will: •Connect to Internet •Search for information •Select information •Copy information to WP document •Print.

As a birthday treat for your friend, your friend's parents are sending you and him on a trip to London to see his favourite football team. You will be staying with your friend's relatives in London and his parents have asked you to use the Internet to find:

Task 1
The cost of a return flight from an airport close to where you live to London. You will be travelling on Friday and returning on Monday.
Task 2
Tickets for the match.
Task 3
A map of the London Underground.
Task 4
The sterling value of €120.00.

Task 5

Copy the information found for each task to a word processing document and save the file as **FOOTIETRIP**.

Task 6

Print one copy of the file.